THE NEWSPAPER

AN ALTERNATIVE TEXTBOOK

★ ★ ★ ★

J. Rodney Short and Bev Dickerson

★   ★ ★ ★ ★   ★

Fearon Teacher Aids
Carthage, Illinois

D0068074

The authors are grateful to the Corpus Christi (Texas) Caller-Times
for permission to reproduce the clippings that are used in the text.

Educational Consultant: Margaret Cross
Editor: Bonnie Bernstein
Designer: Susan True
Cover designer: Bill Nagel
Illustrator: Mary Ann Schildknecht

ISBN–0–8224–4661–8
Library of Congress Catalog Card Number: 79–54759
Printed in the United States of America.
1.9 8

THE NEWSPAPER

AN ALTERNATIVE TEXTBOOK

CONTENTS

1 **THE NEWSPAPER:** An Alternative Textbook   1

2 **SKILL-BUILDERS AND LONG-TERM PROJECTS:** Introductory Activities   13

3 **THE FRONT PAGE:** Investigating Today's Headlines   21

4 **EDITORIALS AND COMMENTARY:** Distinguishing Fact and Opinion   31

5 **COMMUNITY NEWS:** Focusing on People and Culture   41

6 **THE BUSINESS WORLD:** Analyzing Today's Economy   49

7 **SPORTS SCENE:** Scouting the Action   61

8 **NEWSPAPER FEATURES:** Exploring Diverse Interests   71

9 **DISPLAY ADVERTISING:** Questioning the Sponsors   81

10 **CLASSIFIED ADVERTISING:** Buying Wisely   89

11 **VITAL STATISTICS:** Understanding Facts and Figures   97

12 **THE FUNNY PAGES:** Enjoying Comics and Puzzles   105

GLOSSARY: Standard Terms   111

ACTIVITY INDEX   115

1

THE NEWSPAPER
An Alternative Textbook

Most teachers would agree that the ideal textbook for the comprehensive secondary classroom would be socially relevant, geared for low-level readers, informative and appealing on a wide range of subjects, and continually updated. If you are willing to forego the conveniences of compact size and a sturdy cover, you already have such a textbook at hand—the daily newspaper.

The newspaper is an excellent tool for motivating students to learn in spite of themselves. Even the most resistant readers will turn eagerly to the sports pages, the entertainment listings, or the front page account of a catastrophic event. *The Newspaper: An Alternative Textbook* is designed to take advantage of this interest in two ways—by using the newspaper as a reading incentive and as a source of practical information about the world at large. The activities in this handbook involve students in both the form and the content of the news as it appears in newspapers.

The newspaper functions like a school without walls. It provides students with a panoramic view of their lives in the context of the community around them. For the restless student, it is immediate and concise. For the teacher, it offers a vast data pool for studies of the social and physical sciences. It requires student readers to muster and refine their language arts skills in order to take advantage of its many resources. Furthermore, the newspaper is inexpensive, accessible, and wide in subject scope.

It has often been argued that the people who write and edit conventional, highly refined textbooks derive more educational benefit from the experience than do the students who read the end product. The newspaper, however, provides students with raw, unfiltered data that they must process themselves. And the experience of gathering, assessing, distilling, interpreting, summarizing, and translating data helps students develop analytical skills that influence their abilities to learn in the classroom and to make practical and value-oriented decisions in their everyday lives.

Like other media that report on the fast-breaking events of the real world, the newspaper is imperfect; at times it can be prone to bias, misinformation, distortion, and sensationalism. After all, a newspaper is the product of editors and writers who, like the rest of us, are subject to human error. Sometimes unintentionally, and sometimes not, opinion is mistaken for fact. Therefore, *The Newspaper: An Alternative Textbook* includes activities that teach students to be more discerning users of the newspaper and other media. Such discretionary skills can only prove useful to students in their scholastic, practical, and private lives.

LEARNING LEVELS

Any student who is reading comfortably on the third grade level or better will be able to work with most daily newspapers. The activities in this book are designed to appeal to a wide range of students, from the least sophisticated to the most mature, from intermediate grammar school children to middle and high school students and adults. You will naturally want to focus on those activities which are most appropriate to the age, ability, maturity level, and interests of your students, and which reflect your overall objectives for the class.

Intermediate Grades

For many years, fifth and sixth grade teachers have used the newspaper in the classroom to supplement students' coursework in language arts and social studies. The activities in this book can be used to develop or expand such a program at the intermediate level. An extensive newspaper study can also provide the core of an enrichment semester for an accelerated intermediate class. Gifted children in such classes are usually only eleven or twelve years of age, and it is often inadvisable to advance them too rapidly. An enrichment semester involving activities like the ones in this handbook will give these children an opportunity to consolidate their gains, integrate their skills, and mature a little before they go on to the next grade level.

Middle or Junior High School Grades

The newspaper can be used to supplement coursework in language arts and social studies for middle school students also. Those students whose reading levels remain at third, fourth, or low fifth and whose computation skills are weak usually gain the most benefit from newspaper-related activities. Often these students have become greatly discouraged and disinterested in learning in general. The newspaper offers them a source of motivation—the opportunity to select topics of study that really interest them. As these students accumulate information about their chosen topics, their resources for concrete thought and conversation will also increase. And their self-esteem should improve proportionally. For as learning becomes less painful, knowledge is more easily acquired and more frequently rewarded with confidence. Needless to say, students at a more accelerated level should also be encouraged to read and study the newspaper for their pleasure and educational benefit.

High School Grades and Adult Classes

High school students experiencing reading difficulties can use the newspaper in the same way as middle school students. Those students who, on the other hand, demonstrate average or high levels of achievement can use newspaper material to probe complex subjects and issues in greater depth. In doing so, they will learn to use skills and methodology applicable at the college and professional levels.

Adults coming to the classroom to learn English in ESL programs will find the newspaper a practical guide. For them, the newspaper provides a controlled vocabulary, topics appropriate to their more mature interests, and information about the mainstream society.

CLASSROOM MANAGEMENT AND THE NEWSPAPER

Classroom management will depend largely on the arrangements you make for providing your students with newspapers. If you provide each student with a semester's worth of daily issues you are likely to have more problems with storage and disposal than if you provide two months' worth of community weeklies. Even the most trivial management considerations, such as preventing students from knocking elbows as they turn pages, require a degree of foresight and planning. Take the following factors into consideration as you plan ways to manage the classroom activities:

the maturity level of students

the characteristic behavior of students

classroom layout

display space

the extent of library resources

the extent of the newspaper study

prior student experience with the newspaper

These considerations will also guide you in deciding on the appropriateness of the following suggestions for selecting, distributing, storing, and handling newspapers in your particular classroom situation.

Selecting a Newspaper

The newspapers available for your use might include a community weekly, a community daily, a metropolitan daily (morning or evening edition, or both), and a school newspaper. If you have such an extensive choice, the evening edition of a metropolitan daily will best enable you to take advantage of the activities suggested in this book. It will provide the optimal coverage for most newspaper activities, besides affording you the opportunity to study the paper the evening before it is distributed to the class. If you have the funds, provide each student with a personal issue daily for at least one month, and begin distribution a full week before you begin your class study of the newspaper. Following the first month, provide only a few issues daily that the class can use for group work and for comparison with their original month's data base.

This would be an ideal arrangement. However, your choice will be determined largely by the particular newspapers published in your community, the policies of your school district, the available funds, and the amount of time you plan to devote to the class study. (At this point you may wish to read the chapter sections carefully, tentatively select the activities you would like to use, and review the newspapers available to you with those activities in mind.)

Consider the characteristic features of the various kinds of newspapers. You will probably want to discount the school newspaper because it is overly simplistic, too periodic (comes out biweekly, monthly, or once a semester), and far too limited in coverage. A community paper might be appropriate for a limited study, since it will carry a high percentage of news about people and events in your town, and you can rely on its being geared to a third or fourth grade reading level. Community papers are published in small cities with populations under 100,000, suburbs or districts of large metropolitan areas, and various other communities. They usually emphasize local coverage.

Newspapers published in state capitals and larger cities will naturally offer more state-wide news, and probably more national and world coverage, but less information about local events. Metropolitan papers are written at a slightly more difficult reading level than community papers, and they are distributed daily to people in a wide geographical area extending far beyond the metropolitan limits. And finally, the newspapers that are read all over the nation and the world—among them the *New York Times,* the *Christian Science Monitor,* and the *Wall Street Journal*—of course require a still higher reading level than either community or large metropolitan papers.

Although you will want to select one paper for most of the activity projects suggested, it might be interesting to expose the class to examples of each of these kinds of newspapers during the course of the study. In addition, you may want to bring in a few issues of the local shoppers' guide, papers published by subculture groups, and other special interest sheets. They can be used to supplement or contrast with the newspaper under close study.

If sufficient funds have not already been provided in your supplies budget, consider alternative means of funding the class study. You can ask students to pay for their own newspapers, or, if this is not possible or desirable, you can solicit the sponsorship of the PTA and other community service organizations. If all else fails, you can use once-read papers donated by a faithful group of thirty-plus volunteer households. (It should not be difficult to collect newspapers from people who would otherwise have the nuisance of recycling them themselves.)

Lack of money need not be a serious obstacle to your study. Don't forget that newspaper publishers often will give reduced rates to a school project and may also be willing to provide students with old wire copy, guided tours of offices, guest speakers, and more. The circulation manager of the paper can be a valuable contact.

Distributing and Storing Papers

As you devise a method for acquiring newspapers, keep in mind that if you have several classes working with you during the day, the students from the various classes can share one set of papers—that is, if the students are fairly mature, thoughtful people. Newspapers do become easily disordered and thereby lose some of their appeal.

No matter which paper you select, the prospect of receiving thirty-plus copies at once—perhaps every day for a week—can seem overwhelming. One way to maintain order and organization is to "file" the newspapers in open cartons. Look for discarded boxes that are the approximate size of a folded newspaper; label each front panel with the names and dates of the papers stored in that box.

Newspapers can also be stored in grocery bags. Ask each student to label the top edge of a grocery bag with his or her name, followed by the name of the newspaper and the date of the first issue. Subsequent issues will be inserted and listed by date until the bag is filled to capacity. Insist that any issues not in use be stored away neatly in the bags. If the newspapers are being used cooperatively by more than one class, assign a number code to each student, repeating the code for each class. Then have students label their bags by number rather than by name. Have the first student to use each newspaper write the corresponding code number on each section so that the paper can be easily reassembled at the end of the class period.

Ask the delivery person to stack the papers near the classroom door each day. As the students arrive in the morning, they can pick up a copy of the paper, find their assigned bags, and get settled. While you are handling the mechanics of getting the day started, your students can peruse the paper and read their favorite columns. If the papers are used cooperatively by several classes, the students in the later classes should form the habit of picking up their coded bags as they enter the room and settling down to read the current issue while the class assembles.

When your classroom study is over, ask your students to bundle up their used newspapers and take them to a recycling depot.

Handling Papers

Newspapers are cumbersome, and most adults cannot handle them with much grace; imagine thirty or more adolescents grappling with papers in the confines of your seating arrangement. On the first day, therefore, take time to teach your students how to fold the newspaper with a minimum of frustration and fumbling. Use the following steps to explain this procedure:

1. Choose the section you want to read and remove it from the rest of the folded paper.
2. Set the other sections aside.
3. Choose a page and turn to it.
4. Fold the paper back along its natural crease.
5. Fold it in half again horizontally to expose the desired article.

Students may need to practice this procedure three or four times before you go on. Then have them choose another page to read, folding and refolding in this same way. After they have finished reading, have them refold the section to its original order, and then refold it back with the rest of the issue.

Locating a particular item in the paper can also be confusing to the novice reader. To simplify this task, call students' attention to the section designation usually found in the upper right corner of each sheet (for example, "A," "B," "C," or "D"). Within each section each page has a number. You might ask the students, for practice, to find "page 5 in section B." Once they can use section and page numbers easily, move on to column number. Tell the students that columns are numbered from left to right on each page. Ask them to find "page 7 in section C, column 2." If your students are having difficulty with this operation, you may want to repeat it several times.

WHAT YOU WILL FIND IN THIS BOOK

A number of general focus activities are presented in Chapter 2. These are designed to be used as skill-builders or long-term projects as various times during your class study. Each of the remaining chapters focuses on one section of the newspaper and contains an informative introduction for the teacher, a section survey to be conducted by the students independently or as a class, follow-up findings to be compiled after the survey, and section activities to explore the diverse features of each newspaper section. At the end of the book is a glossary of standard terms for your convenience.

Section Survey

Each section survey is intended to orient the students to a particular subject area of the newspaper. The format of the survey has been standardized throughout and geared to the reading and computation skills level of the middle or junior high school student. Therefore if you are teaching intermediate students, you may wish to make some modifications.

Each section survey begins with several probing questions, followed by detailed procedural guidelines to help the students compile data on and receive insight into the questions. Any one of the section surveys could form the basis of a provocative social studies discussion.

Follow-up Findings

The follow-up findings provide data for comparative analysis or corroboration of the section survey findings. Some are designed to enable students to explore further and to make a more detailed statistical analysis of one facet of the survey. But for the most part, these activities are fun projects that take the students out of the classroom or bring visitors in—for the purpose of reinforcing what the students have learned from the newspaper. Follow-up findings can be pursued by students at every level.

Assignments

Each section includes a writing assignment designed to familiarize students further with particular journalistic styles of writing as well as to develop their language arts skills. Many assignments are the culmination of a focusing activity; most require research or field work to some degree. When you are assigning stories and features, suggest that your students clip representative articles to use as format samples. Students are encouraged to regard their assignments as real reporters' assignments, and to consider the final draft of an article a contribution to a class newspaper section. Students at any level can handle the writing.

Section Activities

Numerous interdisciplinary activities follow the writing assignment in each chapter. Read each activity carefully before you use it in class, since some explore issues (such as community segregation) that may be too sensitive for your particular classroom situation. Make sure that any activities you select are appropriate for or can be adapted to the age, maturity, and skills level of your students. The chart on page 10 will aid your selection.

STYLE MODELS

The section assignments and activities require that students write many different kinds of newspaper articles and features during the course of their study. However, before they undertake any writing assignments, it is advisable to offer them some instruction in the use of conventional journalistic formats. Described below are the *inverted*

Activities Suitable for Three Learning Levels

SECTION ACTIVITIES	INTER-MEDIATE LEVEL	MIDDLE OR JR.HIGH LEVEL	HIGH SCHOOL OR ADULT LEVEL
Skill-Builders and Long-Term Projects	1, 2, 3, 4, 5, 7, 8	1, 2, 4, 5, 6, 7, 8, 9	1, 6, 7, 8, 9
The Front Page	10, 11, 12, 13, 15, 16, 17, 18	10, 11, 12, 13, 14, 15, 16, 17, 18	10, 11, 12, 14, 15, 17, 18
Editorials and Commentary	19, 20, 21, 22, 23, 24	19, 20, 21, 22, 23, 24	19, 20, 21, 22, 23, 24
Community News	26, 27	25, 26, 27, 28	25, 27, 28
The Business World	29, 31	29, 30, 31, 32, 35	29, 30, 31, 32, 33, 34, 35
Sports Scene	36, 39, 40, 41	36, 37, 39, 40, 41	37, 38, 39, 40, 41
Newspaper Features and Magazines	42, 43, 45	42, 43, 44, 45	42, 43, 44, 45
Display Advertising	46, 47	46, 47, 48, 49	46, 48, 49
Classified Advertising	50, 51, 52, 53	50, 51, 52, 53, 54	50, 51, 52, 53, 54
Vital Statistics	55, 56, 57, 58, 59	55, 56, 57, 58, 59	55, 58, 59
The Funny Pages	63, 64	60, 61, 62, 63, 64, 65	60, 61, 62, 65

pyramid, the format used for reportorial pieces, and the *editorial rocket,* the format used for commentary. The *Who? Chart* is a handy device for amassing and organizing story material.

Inverted Pyramid

Have your students read several straight news stories before you introduce and diagram the inverted pyramid. Point out that the most important information in a news story is found in the first paragraph (called the *lead*), which will usually tell who did what, when, where, how and why. The details of the story are then reported in descending order of importance, inverted pyramid style. Finally ask the students to look again at some of the news items they have read to see how this works.

Inverted Pyramid

lead

most important element

least important element

Editorial Rocket

Explain to the students that the structure of an editorial is similar to a rocket ready for blast-off. The body of the rocket represents the opinion the writer wishes to launch; the legs of the gantry surrounding the rocket are the facts and arguments that support the opinion; and the flames at the base of the rocket show the conclusion that the writer hopes will launch the opinion and fire the reader into agreement and action.

Editorial Rocket

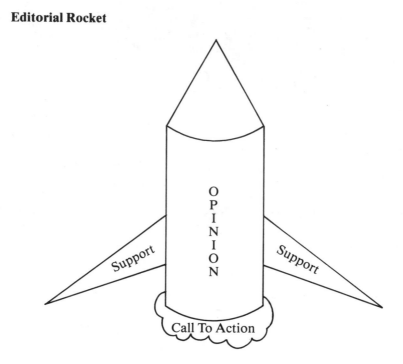

Who? Chart

A comprehensive news story or feature contains answers to all the following questions: Who? What? Where? When? How? Why? If students chart these questions at the outset of a writing assignment, they will be able to identify and organize their ideas and check for content omissions once they have written a draft of the article.

Who? Chart

Who?	
What?	
Where?	
When?	
How?	
Why?	

2

SKILL-BUILDERS AND LONG-TERM PROJECTS
Introductory Activities

Some activities in this section extend through an entire unit, requiring at least a semester to complete, whereas others are less complex and can be repeated for each newspaper section study. Select those which are appropriate to your class's learning needs and objectives, and begin them at the outset of your first section study, the Front Page.

1. Find Your Way Around

This is a newspaper scavenger hunt—an entertaining way of getting your students to familiarize themselves with the general layout of the newspaper. The first scavenger list should contain items that students must hunt for in the entire newspaper. Later scavenger lists should focus on the detailed offerings of the individual section that is under current study by the class.

Hold back the first delivery of class newspapers until you have had a chance to go through the edition yourself. (If you are able to subscribe to the evening edition of a daily paper, then you have a made-to-order situation for this activity.) For the scavenger hunt it is preferable to have a paper for each student and to let students work independently. However, if there are not enough papers to go around, cooperative groups will work well enough.

After you have scavenged the paper yourself for ideas, draw up a lengthy list of items for which the students must hunt in the paper the next day. The first list should include standard features and designations used in your particular newspaper—ears, index, datelines, banner, section heads and codes, masthead, and so on. (You will find these and other features included in the Glossary at the back of the book.) It should also include details from articles, features, and ads that are well-distributed throughout the paper. Here is a standard list to which you can add items from representative material found in your newspaper.

Find Your Way Around

How fast can you find your way around the newspaper? Locate these items, circle them in your paper, and check them off on the list:

__ the *ears* (information boxes in the top corners of the front page)
__ the *banner* (the newspaper nameplate across the front page)
__ the *index* (listing of contents and pages, and sections and section codes)
__ five *wire service* designations (UPI, AP, Reuters)
__ a *political cartoon*
__ the *banner headline* (lead-story headline under banner)
__ five *datelines* (first copy line under a headline, which tells date and place of report)
__ the business section head
__ the editorial section code (assigned letter or number)
__ a travel ad
__ an ad for a used Chevrolet

___ the best supermarket buy on chicken
___ the net change in Exxon's stock that day
___ the averages for a star (football, basketball, or baseball) player
___ the *masthead*
___ the name of a made-for-TV movie
___ the most expensive symphony seats
___ an opinion column by the newspaper publisher

2. Where in the World?

Keep a large map of the world, a world atlas, and a globe on display during the newspaper study. Always ask your students to report on the datelines of articles they read, then to pinpoint where each event took place on the map and the globe. (If a student cannot readily find a location on the world map, help him or her consult the world atlas. Once a place has been located on the atlas map, the student should be able to find its corresponding location easily on the world map and globe.)

Conduct a brief geography lesson on foreign countries of importance in the news. When it is relevant, discuss the role of important neighbors in a news event. Consider how geographic and environmental characteristics of a nation affect the social, economic, and political conditions.

3. Spider and Fly

Spider and Fly is a game that provides students with practice in recognizing and recalling significant details. It can be used frequently during the newspaper study as a reading comprehension activity.

Select a news article and make a copy for each student. Delete and change words in the original article. At the start of the game, direct the students to read their copies and attend closely to the details; then ask them to cover their articles while you read your altered version aloud. Each time a student recognizes a change, he or she "attacks" (as a spider attacks a fly caught in its web) by calling out "no," then providing the correct word, phrase, or date from memory. The students' challenges should be checked against the original.

4. Word Watching: Synonyms

Reporters get most of their information from what people tell them, and often what people have to say is news in itself. If reporters used the verb *said* every time they needed to quote a person or attribute information to a source, journalistic style would be rather repetitious. Instead, a good news writer uses many synonyms in reporting what people say. The synonyms frequently provide a certain connotation as well as needed variety. Discuss the connotations of such words as *accused, conceded, demanded, parried, denied,* and *argued.* Any one of these words might be substituted for the literal *said.* Ask your students to note other non-descript verbs and their more connotative synonyms. Compile a class list over the duration of the study. Headings on the list might include *said, died, won, lost, saw, questioned,* and *went to.*

5.   Word Watching: Vocabulary

When a student encounters an unfamiliar word in the newspaper, have him or her write it on an index card along with the sentence in which it was used, then look up the word in the dictionary. If the dictionary definition is comprehensible to the student, he or she should copy it on the reverse side of the index card, then file the card alphabetically in a box that you provide. If the definition is too complicated, offer a simplified version yourself. Admonish the class to watch for new words throughout the newspaper study. From time to time, quiz individuals or the entire class on their new vocabulary.

6.   Dictionary Update

Occasionally a student will encounter a word in the newspaper and be unable to find it in the classroom dictionary. The word may in fact be a very new word, or one coined by a journalist. Ask your students to write undefined words on index cards along with the sentences in which they are used (or paragraph, if a sentence does not provide enough of a context), then to file them alphabetically. From time to time, encourage the class to define the indexed words from their contexts in sentences. Examples of words of ambiguous origin or unusual and unfamiliar usage might be: crunch *(noun),* clout *(noun),* shuttle diplomacy, and nukes.

At the end of the newspaper study, discuss how new words are assimilated into our language. Ask your students to conduct family surveys to find out about words that are acceptable and commonly used today that were unknown twenty-five or fifty years ago. Use the indexed words to compile an updated dictionary supplement to keep alongside the standard classroom dictionary.

7.   Captive Captions

Ask your students to clip all the photographs and accompanying captions from the newspaper section with which the class is currently
working. Then have them cut off the captions. Provide students with
large manilla envelopes in which to put their scrambled sets of pictures
and captions, and have each student trade with a partner. After the
partners have reassembled the sets, the combinations should be
checked for accuracy by the original clipper.

Post amusing mismatches on a bulletin board. Ask the students who
have mismatched captions and photos why their mismatches made
good—or comical—sense to them. Discuss how ambiguous language
and words with double meanings make some captions seem appropriate or clever in a mistaken context. Underscore the importance of
writing with precision in order to prevent misconceptions.

8.   Series Reports

At the outset of your study of the newspaper, you may want to assign
each student the task of preparing a "series report," to be presented in
installments throughout the period of study. Distribute a duplicated list
of topics that you feel are appropriate and of interest to your students.
Don't hesitate to approve reasonable alternatives from individuals who
are anxious to write on other appropriate subjects. Your list of suggested topics might read like this:

actions or activities of the President

environmental problems and solutions

research and developments in scientific fields

new services, projects, or activities in your community

surveys of public opinion on local referendums, or state and national
issues

political or social changes taking place in another country

a social problem facing a group of people in the U.S.

After students have declared their series report topics, hand out a
task sheet like the one following that outlines the sequence and descriptions of installments due for the report. As with other activities
offered in this handbook, tailor the assignments to the abilities of your
students.

Series Report Installments

1.   Clip all articles that relate to your topic. Summarize each one. If you find material from borrowed resources that cannot be clipped, note the head and dateline, and write a brief synopsis of the article.
2.   Clip pictures, cartoons, maps, and other illustrations that contribute information to your topic.
3.   Write a two page report on the historical background of your topic based on library research.
4.   Locate an address for a person who is said to be an authority on your topic. Write a letter to this person describing your work, and request additional specific information.
5.   Find two articles in news magazines that deal with this topic. Write a brief report on each. Include the name of the magazine, the date of issue, and the pages you read.
6.   If possible, find a book on the topic. Read it and write a brief report. Be sure to note the author, name of book, date of publication, and publisher.
7.   If possible, find out how the topic has been treated in the press of another country. Add this information to your file.
8.   Review any TV programs dealing with this matter. Write a brief report on the content of the program, and note the apparent point of view of the narrator. Include the date, time, name of the program, and any other pertinent information.
9.   Review your cumulative material and prepare a final summary. Include a statement of your own well-informed opinion on the topic.

Assign point values to each installment and indicate the total points required for each letter grade. If you like, draw up a contract with each student which includes the date due for each installment.

9.   Political Profiles

Suggest that your students be responsible for knowing the names and voting records of their elected representatives to the state assembly and to the U.S. Congress. Label the outside of a file folder with the name of each representative, his or her party affiliation, office, term of election, date for future reelection, and the key issues with which he or she is associated. Place these folders along a chalk tray, or display them in another convenient place.

   Instruct your students to clip newspaper articles and other information about these people for the files. Tell them to include pictures of the representatives and any promotional literature they are able to obtain from the county or state political party office.

Draw your students' attention to the differing treatments of the same politician. Some representatives may seem fairly inactive. At times the local press may be harshly critical, at other times very flattering. Encourage students to search through the library's recent issues of major national newspapers such as the *New York Times, Christian Science Monitor,* or *Wall Street Journal* for information on one or more of their elected representatives written from the perspective of out-of-town or out-of-state journalists. The comparative distance of these reporters may enable them to be less subjective. Notes about such articles should be added to the classroom files.

As the clippings accumulate and the students become more familiar with their representatives, review the profiles. Ask students to characterize their representatives at the state and national levels. Have them decide what kinds of people and interest groups are best represented by each office holder, in the light of the analysis in the political profiles.

A kit of materials has been assembled for teachers, students, and community citizens who want to profile members of Congress. The kit provides specific guidelines and bibliographic references as well as two sample profiles on past members of Congress. The kit can be obtained for $2.00 postpaid. Write for the Public Citizen Congressional Profile Kit, P.O. Box 19404, Washington, D.C. 20036.

3

THE FRONT PAGE
Investigating Today's Headlines

Traditionally the front page of a newspaper carries the articles and pictures that its editors consider most newsworthy on any particular day. These may be items of local, national, or international significance. Front page stories are usually factual and informative and—in order to have the immediate quality of "news"—most current. They chronicle the day's events and developments, and report the latest word from reliable sources.

The front page may be a single sheet in a very small newspaper or several sheets folded within one another to form the entire front section of a larger paper. Whatever its size, the front page is designed to attract the reader's eye at the newsstand.

To sell their papers, front page editors may select and display the news of the day with the intention of attracting the reader. Some front pages contain feature stories or columns. Others contain the lurid details of a violent crime or fatal accident. Others rely on a longstanding reputation for responsible and comprehensive coverage of diverse news events, and do little more than assign precedence to stories on the front page. The final selection of stories and their strategic arrangement on the front page varies a great deal from paper to paper and provides a clue to each paper's intellectual stance and readership. Students should be made aware of these distinctions.

SECTION SURVEY

Provide each student with a front page or front page section of the newspaper to which the class subscribes. If possible, distribute copies from several days' issues (perhaps a week's worth), so that only a few students will be working on the same day's paper. After they have read all the front page articles, ask them to conduct a section survey using the following questions and procedural guidelines:

Front Page Survey

What is the primary focus of the front page news? Does your newspaper highlight local, state, national, or international events? What are its lead-story topics?

1.   Make a topical list of every article (news, feature, or filler) on your front page or in your front page section. Regroup your list under general headings such as Crime, Natural Disaster, Politics, Human Interest, Weather, Violence (includes wars, uprisings, fights), Government, Progress, Ecology. Note your lead story—the article with the banner headline.

2.   Designate where the news event occurred using the following code: L for Local, S for State, N for National, and I for International.

3.   Note the date on which the story is reported. Occasionally the dateline of an article will predate the issue in which it is published.

4.   Combine your list with the lists of the other students. First, tally the total number of news items found in the front pages of the papers issued during the survey period. (If more than one student has surveyed a single issue, those students should select a representative

from among themselves to contribute one list.) Divide the number of articles by the number of individual issues to find the average number of front page articles per day.

5.   Tally the overall number of items that fall under each general heading. Divide each of these numbers by the cumulative number of front page articles in order to find the percentage of articles per day that fall under each general heading. Draw a bar graph to compare the percentages. Note any outstanding ratios, such as Government to Human Interest: 3 to 1.

Sample Bar Graph

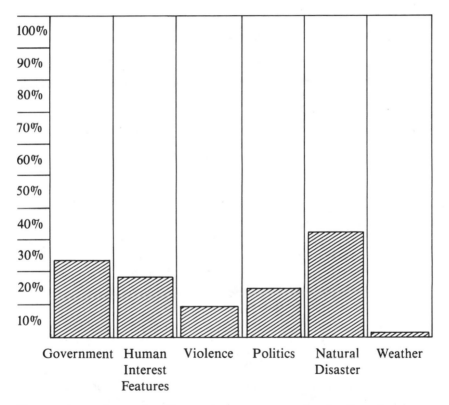

Bar graphs can be used to illustrate percentages and ratios for other section survey data.

6.   Using the same procedure, derive percentages and ratios for the locales of items published during the survey period. Draw a bar graph. Note any outstanding ratios, such as National to Local: 5 to 2.

7. Tally the number of lead stories that fall under each general heading. Derive percentages and ratios for lead topics on the front pages of papers issued during the survey period. Draw a bar graph. Note any outstanding ratios. Compare the percentages and ratios of the lead stories under each general heading to the percentage of articles under each general heading.

After the class has conducted its survey, discuss the findings in the context of the questions posed at the outset of the survey. Your data analysis should provide the answers.

FOLLOW-UP FINDINGS

In the front page survey, students should have generalized their observations about the content of the front page of a newspaper.

As a follow-up to the survey, invite a staff journalist from the paper to which the class subscribes, or from another local paper, to visit the classroom and answer queries about the criteria for selecting front page news stories.

In preparation for the visit, ask each student to compose three questions. Give the questions to the visitor several days in advance so that he or she can be prepared to provide answers and discussion. During the visit, encourage students to take notes on new information the guest speaker may contribute to their survey generalizations about front page news. Modifications may be in order.

Students can check their survey findings by completing a simple follow-up study. Have them record corresponding data for current incoming papers (include as many issues as were in the original set), and compare their findings. Unless an unusually serious news occurrence has offset the balance of daily coverage during one of the two periods under scrutiny, the topical and regional distribution of lead stories and articles should remain about the same for both sets of front pages.

Students can also conduct a comparative survey of several other newspapers, compiling data for three or more consecutive issues of each paper. Compute, interpret, and compare these follow-up findings in class.

ASSIGNMENT: Cover a News Conference

The front page regularly features a report of a presidential news conference, and probably such an event will have taken place during the period covered in your class survey. However, news conferences are by no means limited to the President of the United States. Other city, state, and federal officials call them to inform constituents about the sponsorship of legislative bills or public events, or the monitoring of an emergency situation. Occasionally conferences will be granted to the press by an award recipient or a returning celebrity. It is quite likely that the lead story on the front page of every issue surveyed by the class was a composite of information gathered at a news conference of one sort or another.

Have your students reread articles that cover news conferences; then have them characterize the conferences. Discuss the tenor of the questions and responses. Ask the class to remark on the attitude of the reporter to the conference speaker. Frequently the hostility or sympathy of the reporter will be manifested by the questions and responses he or she chose to include in the article. At times the reporter will be subjective to the extent that he or she will insert a description of the speaker's demeanor during the conference. Have the students check national news magazines that covered the same news conference. Ask them to report and investigate any differences they find in the coverage.

Invite the principal or another school administrator to hold a news conference for the class. Provide him or her with a list of students' questions well in advance of the date. Suggest that the occasion of your conference be an impending announcement, since announcements are frequently the motive for which government leaders call *their* news conferences. Then assign your student reporters their first story —coverage of a live news conference.

If an administrator is not available, officiate the conference yourself. Inform students that you will assume the identity of someone currently in the news. (Specify the person.) Once familiarized with that person's activities and affiliations, plan a hypothetical announcement that he or she might make at an upcoming news conference.

Before the day of the conference, have your students propose and discuss appropriate issues on which they want to query the guest.

Research in the school and local newspapers will probably define or clarify the speaker's stance on some of these issues. Ask each student to submit several questions that the speaker can plan to address. Have the students keep copies of the questions for themselves. Then compile the list of questions and turn them over to the speaker.

On the day of the conference, instruct students to take notes. Appoint a moderator to recognize "reporters" when they rise to ask questions. Appoint another student to thank the guest when the designated time period is over.

After the conference, encourage students to compare notes, check quotes, and fill in any information they may have missed. Then discuss the conference. What did the guest say that was news? What was the most important or unexpected statement he or she made? The latter question should provide students with the lead sentence for the first paragraph of their news stories, and might also be rephrased as a headline. Before the students begin to write, review the inverted pyramid style that reporters use to structure their articles. (See page 11.) Encourage students to regularly headline their stories.

SECTION ACTIVITIES

10. Making the Front Page

Engage your class in a cooperative venture—the production of a front page or front page section made up of their individual contributions. First appoint a staff of front page editors to decide on the number of articles, the ratio of topics (see page 23), and the scope, or geographic range, of the places to be featured in the articles. The editors may want to distribute assignments according to the subject matter and scope of the real newspaper. If so, have them refer to the class's section survey findings.

The editors should assign each student reporter a topic and a locale. Using the Who? Chart, the students can collect the necessary information to write their articles. After final drafts have been typed and submitted, instruct the editorial staff to plan, layout, and assemble an oversized front page or front page section featuring the class contributions. If there is room, include one or two past assignments covering the class press conference.

11. A Measure of Importance

Students have surveyed the *frequency* with which general topics and events are reported, but they have not yet determined the *extent* of the coverage of individual items on the front page.

Ask your students to recheck the major topics reported on the front page during the survey period. Instruct them to measure and count the number of column inches devoted to each of these topics during that period. Have them compute percentages and construct a bar graph to illustrate their findings. Discuss how the number of days on which a topic is reported constitutes another variable for measuring the extent of coverage of that topic.

12. Tour a Newspaper Office

Schedule a tour of your local newspaper office. Arrange a time when a staff member can meet and talk with students to explain the steps in news gathering, writing, editing, copy editing, production, and circulation. If possible, arrange to visit the areas where typesetting and printing take place. Watch the compositors, presses, and folding machines in operation.

Sample Sequence Chart

news event happens	reporter covers event	reporter writes story	city editor approves story
1.	2.	3.	4.
copy reader edits story	copy to typesetter	proof-reader corrects galleys	layout editor arranges pages
5.	6.	7.	8.
graphic artist makes paste-up	printer makes plates	web press prints, collates, cuts, folds	papers sent out for delivery
9.	10.	11.	12.

Following the visit to the newspaper office, students can assemble a sequence chart to show how a news event becomes a published article. If the class cannot visit a newspaper office, use the chart on the preceding page to explain the process.

13.   History in the Making

Ask each student to select the one or two news items from the front page he or she has been working with that will be historically significant twenty-five years from now. Ask students to figure out how old they will be in twenty-five years and to imagine what their concerns might be at that time. Then ask students to clip one or two articles that they think will be important in a year or two years. The clipped articles can be sealed in a box along with the names of the students who selected them. The box can be labeled "to be opened in . . . ." Open the box with your students after the designated time interval and examine the contents. How many stories have been totally forgotten, and how many deal with issues that are still vital? If you will be with the class for one school year only, arrange to open the box at the end of the year.

14.   Past Pages

This activity gives students the opportunity to place the events of the day in a historical perspective. Initially students will need to look again at the list of front page topics (including the datelines) which they compiled in their section survey. This list may encompass topics which appeared on the front page of one issue, or many consecutive issues over a designated period of time. Whatever the time period has been, the historical time period must be the same length. Working in groups of three or four, students should select dates (perhaps for the same month as the current study period) five years, ten years, or another staggered number of years in the past. The availability of microfilm or microfiche of the newspapers for these years may limit the choice.

Each work group then reviews the papers for its study period and conducts the same section survey as they did earlier for the current period. The groups will be looking for the major issues and the places where these events took place.

As each group completes its survey, the findings are mounted on a time line near the date of the survey period. Discuss the cumulative findings in the context of these questions:

In which years was there more interest in national issues? In world issues? What events might have precipitated such interest?

Which issues, if any, are still of interest or importance?

15. Secondhand History

Ask each of your students to select a historical event that took place within living memory. Such events might include the attack on Pearl Harbor, the McCarthy hearings, and the assassination of President Kennedy. Have the students first confirm the years in which their chosen events took place, then set about locating primary sources —people who were adults at the time.

Instruct your students to prepare five or six good questions before they proceed with an interview. Once they have obtained first-hand information about the historical event from an interview with an adult who experienced it (or news of it), ask them to write a news report. Encourage them to search into other accounts describing the event in order to verify and procure additional details. The assignment is not to report on an interview. Rather, the students are to put themselves in the place of the interviewed person and recount the eventful happenings as if recalling them from first-hand experience. In this way, the story will have the immediacy of news.

16. Weather Watch

A brief summary of the local weather forecast is often found on the front page. Have your students prepare a weather chart for the consecutive issues of the newspaper covered in the section survey. This could be a large calendar with at least 4" × 4" space for each day.

Instruct your students to fill in the date and the forecast for that date. When all the dates have been recorded for the survey period, have your students compute the percentage of daily forecasts for sun, rain, fog, snow, and so on. Keep tabs on the actual weather patterns experienced on the surveyed dates to check the accuracy of the predictions.

17. What's at Stake?

Frequently reporters will cover stories from different angles, depending on their own attitudes or what they expect the readers' interests to be in the particular issue or event. Ask your students to review two or three front page topics that received several days' coverage. Have them note the vantage points or angles from which various writers pursue the facts and details of the same events. Observe which factors and circumstances in the event would affect the various writers in different ways. The location of the writer in relation to the event would be one observable factor in the discussion. The class can collect the stories on one event and note the developments in the depth of coverage as time passes.

Encourage your students to supplement the several days' coverage in their newspapers with coverage in other newspapers and dated publications. Once again, identify and compare angles. Other students may want to collect still more information by interviewing people in the community who were involved in or affected by the issue. For example, if the topic is a snowstorm, students will begin to see that one news article may focus on the statistics of snowfall, accident reports, transportation slowdowns, and similar inconveniences. Yet, an interview with another person may reveal a very different view—that person may enjoy a work-day off, appreciate the beauty of snow-white branches, and see other benefits to the storm.

After students have collected material from other newspapers and from direct interviews, ask each one to write their own news article on the topic. Remind them to follow the inverted pyramid structure and the Who? Chart. The challenge here is to write an unbiased article—to simply report the news.

Later, when they are studying editorials and commentary, students may want to return to their topics and prepare editorials representing their personal viewpoints.

18. It's All in Your Point of View!

To demonstrate to the students that each observer does indeed have a different point of view, you may want to stage this dramatization. Ask two students from another class to come to your room, stage a mock argument, and leave. When they have gone, ask each student to write a news article describing this event. For this exercise, suggest that each person assume a fictitious by-line.

Display the articles on the bulletin board and direct students to read all of them. Promote a discussion with the following questions:

What different points of view are represented?

Are there stylistic differences in the articles?

Why aren't all the articles pretty much the same?

4

EDITORIALS AND COMMENTARY
Distinguishing Fact and Opinion

On the editorial page, the publisher and editors of a newspaper state their opinions about current issues. This page is usually found in the second section of the paper which also contains syndicated columns by nationally popular or controversial journalists. Such columns offer additional commentary or analysis on current news developments. Frequently the editorial page features one or more editorial cartoons which may be the work of a staff person but are more often syndicated. Letters to the editor are usually also found on the editorial page. These letters express the opinions of readers on local and national issues, or on the newspaper's treatment and coverage of those issues. All four kinds of editorial material—editorials, syndicated commentary, cartoons, and letters to the editor—reflect the personal or corporate biases of the writers.

The section which features the editorial page may also present question-and-answer columns, advice columns, book reviews, commentary on lifestyle or human behavior, and other noneditorial material. However, some or all of this material may appear instead in a community news and culture section.

During their study of editorials and commentary in the newspaper, students will learn to sensitize themselves to the use of language in order to distinguish fact and opinion. A simple way to define fact is to note that *all* facts can be verified—by research into records, by precise measurement, or by first-hand experience. If students are uncertain about whether statements they encounter in this study represent fact or opinion, encourage them to assume that they represent opinion until they have verified them as fact.

SECTION SURVEY

Provide each student with an editorial page or section of the newspaper. If possible, provide a month's worth of papers; if not, a week's worth will suffice for comparison. After students have read every feature, ask them to conduct a section survey using the following questions and procedural guidelines:

Editorial Section Survey

On what sorts of issues do editors focus their editorials? Are the issues to which the editors address themselves in your paper local, state, national, or international in scope? Which of the four kinds of editorial material—editorials, syndicated commentary, cartoons, and letters to the editor—receives the most coverage? Do writers of editorials and commentary use language to persuade readers of their opinion? If so, how?

1.   Count the number of items of each kind of editorial material. For each of the four, measure the total number of column inches of material. Draw a pie chart to graph comparisons.

Sample Pie Charts

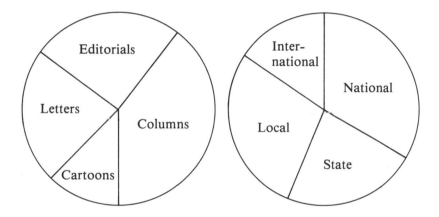

Pie charts can be used to illustrate percentages and ratios for other section survey data.

2.   Combine your findings with members of the class who have surveyed other consecutive issues. Total your column inches for each of the four kinds of editorial material, then divide that measurement by the number of consecutive issues surveyed to determine the average number of column inches per day for each kind of material. Draw a pie chart to graph comparisons. Compare the group chart with your own chart.

3.   List all your editorial material under topical headings. Compute the average coverage devoted to each topic in your particular issue, then in consecutive issues. Draw pie charts to graph comparisons. Read the corresponding front page of your issue and note the extent of news coverage for topics that received extensive editorial coverage.

4.   Use Local, State, National, and International as general headings to define the scope of editorial material. Compute the extent of coverage devoted to the material under each heading in your issue, then in consecutive issues. Draw pie charts to graph comparisons.

5.   Reread the editorials and syndicated commentary. Underline statements that include verifiable facts. Note whether these facts support the viewpoint of the writer.

6.   Circle all the verbs and modifiers (adjectives and adverbs) in at least twenty-five nonfactual statements. Discuss the connotations of these statements with your classmates. Observe how these words influence the way you are beginning to think about the issue on which the columnist is writing.

After the rest of the class has completed the section survey, compare and discuss your findings. Keep in mind the questions posed at the beginning of the survey. Your data analysis should provide the answers.

FOLLOW-UP FINDINGS

Although students are learning to distinguish fact from opinion in writing, it may be more difficult for them to make the distinction in the spoken media. Some of their favorite TV or radio news commentators may editorialize without their being aware of it. Moreover, many television and radio news programs contain a special segment during which an editorial comment on a specific news item is given. From their experience with newspaper editorials, students should be better equipped to evaluate that editorial comment.

These follow-up activities will enable students to sharpen their perceptions of the spoken word as they did the written word in their section survey. By observing the way in which a speaker uses language and introduces certain facts to persuade his or her listeners, the student listeners will be better able to perceive how an imbalance of facts and opinion influences them.

Invite a local government official or another person directly involved with a current local issue to visit the class. Students might choose an item from among those they discussed in their front page study. At this point, the students will also have read several editorials on these issues and thus will have amassed a body of fact and opinion relating to them.

They should narrow their choice down to two or three items and explore the availability of a speaker before making a final selection.

Once the issue is fixed and a speaker has agreed to come, ask your students to prepare a list of questions, which could be given to the guest speaker in advance of the interview. However, if you do provide the speaker with questions in advance, you should make clear to your students that this is not actual journalistic practice. Arrange to have the interview tape-recorded, but be sure you have the permission of the speaker. Conduct the interview as you did the press conference.

Following the session, replay the tape and ask the students to listen very carefully. When someone wishes to point out a factual statement or an opinion, stop the tape and replay that part. Discuss which words suggest fact and which suggest opinion. Have the students make a list of "opinion" words. Encourage your students to recall facts about the issue that they have read elsewhere but that the speaker chose not to mention. Discuss the propaganda term *cardstacking,* the imbalanced or distorted presentation of facts. Underscore the importance of weighing all the facts involved in an issue, not just those presented by a writer or speaker who has taken a particular stance on the issue.

Ask your students to compare the "opinion" words they noted from the tape recording with the "opinion" words they circled in the editorial page or section of their newspapers. Have them consider these questions to guide the comparison:

Do the words on both lists have strong connotations?

Do the words on both lists have the same connotations? (Discuss negative and positive connotation.)

Can you identify any words that are used to support a *pro* stance, or are an argument *for* something?

Do these words support verifiable facts or things you know or believe to be true?

Are there any remaining words that cannot be categorized?

Students will probably notice that some statements appear to be fact although they cannot be verified. These statements may simply strike students as factual because they are based on strong ethical or logical foundations and therefore seem unquestionable.

At this point ask one student to look up the word *truth* in a standard dictionary and read the entire definition to the class. The first or common definition will relate truth to reality or factual evidence; however, as the other meanings are read, students will find that also associated with *true* or *truth* is the concept of belief. Truth is ultimately regarded as reality or facts *as they are perceived by the speaker or writer.*

ASSIGNMENT: Write an Editorial

Ask your students to select an event or issue from those discussed during the study of the front page or the section containing editorials and commentary, then write an editorial giving their own opinion. Review the rocket structure of editorial style. (See pages 11–12.) Suggest that students look again at the editorials they have been reading to remember which ones made them feel strongly about an issue as they read it. Have them pattern their own editorials on these persuasive models if they are having difficulty getting their ideas "launched." Encourage controversy within the class.

After students have written and typed the final drafts of their editorials, appoint a staff of editors to plan, layout, and assemble an oversized editorial page for the class. If there are outstanding contributions, have students submit them on an individual basis to a local newspaper. (If some students prefer to write letters, you might decide to accept letters to the editor of the newspaper under current study as a substitute fulfillment of this assignment.)

SECTION ACTIVITIES

19.   Cartoon Commentary

A study of the political cartoons on the editorial page will offer students an appreciation and understanding of graphic editorials, and will sharpen their visual perception. Ask each student to select a cartoon from his or her editorial section for close scrutiny. Pose these questions in order to guide their observations:

Who or what do the artist's drawings represent? (Specify people, symbolic objects, concepts, metonymical devices.)

What exaggerated features or symbols make clear who or what is represented?

Discuss the language used in the caption. Is there a pun or double meaning? Is there an ironic "quote"?

How does the cartoon comment on an issue currently in the news? Can you find an editorial that verbalizes rather than illustrates the same view on the issue?

20. Dear Editor

It should have been observed by now that on the editorial page, space allowance for certain topics usually reflects the same bias as front page news coverage. Additional survey activity will probably suggest that the same bias extends to the selection of letters to the editor.

Ask your students to assign topical headings to the letters to the editor that appear in the issues covered in the section survey. Have them compute the coverage of each topic and draw a pie chart to graph comparisons. Have them perform the same computations for coverage devoted to materials of particular regional scope (local, state, national, and international) and again draw a pie chart to graph comparisons. Finally, ask your students to compare the pie charts for the letters to the editor with the pie charts for other editorial material surveyed earlier.

Some students may also want to contact the local editor in charge of the letters to the editor section and obtain the following information:

the average number of letters received each day

the average number of letters printed

the criteria for choosing letters for publication

the amount of space allotted to letters regarding issues of particular regional scope

the amount of space allotted to letters regarding issues currently in the front page news

Review the information gleaned from the interview with the editor. Discuss whether or not the information meets the expectations of the class based on its survey findings.

21.   Yours Truly

After carefully looking at the letters to the editor, ask each student to write a letter to one of the newspapers currently under study. First ask the students to look again at the letters in one issue of the newspaper. Pose these questions to guide their observations:

What seems to be the central purpose of each letter?

How many are thoughtful, humorous, angry, satirical, or of another sentiment?

Which letter in this sample is most effective?

Using the most effective letter as a model, each student should write a letter about a current topic of his or her choice.

22.   Analysis of an Analysis

Ask each student to choose a syndicated column featuring an analysis that is particularly interesting to him or her. After the students have reread the columns, ask them to consider the following questions in guiding their analysis of an analysis:

What is the issue being analyzed by the syndicated writer?

What are the alternatives suggested in other readings on the issue?

What are the writer's suggestions?

What facts does the writer choose to include and exclude in order to support his or her conclusions?

Why might the writer have adopted this particular position on the issue?

To answer the final question, the student can talk with others studying the same writer. He or she can research other publications, TV talk shows, and so on, to find out if anyone has uncovered any background information about the writer which explains his or her biases. If not, the librarian may be able to suggest materials that will help students discover where that person really stands on the issues and why.

23.   Who's Who Among the Editors

Most editorial pages carry the masthead for the paper. The masthead usually gives the names of the founder, publisher, and editor-in-chief; where and when the paper is published; subscription rates; and other pertinent editorial information.

Locate the masthead with your students. Ask them to make a list of all the information they can glean from it. Pose the following questions to guide their activity:

How many different titles are listed on the masthead?

How many of the people are men? Women?

Who founded this paper? What do you know about that person or persons? Are there places in the community named after them?

Some students may want to find out more about these key people. Have them write the editor or contact the circulation manager to ask for a brief biographical sketch of each person credited in the masthead, and share this information with the class. Discuss the background characteristics that most of these people have in common. Note what each one did in order to attain his or her position.

Often the founders of newspapers are long dead. Typically they belong to the generations that pioneered locally and founded the towns. Some students may want to form a work group and research the history of your town to find out more about the lives of the founders of the local newspaper. They can then assemble the information in a scrapbook and share it with the entire class. If the people involved were especially colorful, the work group could prepare a short drama depicting several scenes from the biographical material they found.

24. Let's Face Facts

Have each student work with a different set of back issues of the newspaper to locate a news article and an editorial dealing with the same topic. Ask students to read both items, underlining in blue every statement that seems to be fact and in red every statement that seems to be opinion. To guide the activity, ask:

How many factual statements are included in the news item? In the editorial?

How many opinion statements are included in the news item? In the editorial?

How would you compare the factual treatment versus the editorial treatment of the topic in the two items?

5

COMMUNITY NEWS
Focusing on People and Culture

In the past, articles of general interest relating to community cultural events could be found in what were called "The Society Pages." Today, however, community news and features are usually clustered under a section heading such as "View," "Scene," "People," or "Lifestyle." In some newspapers, they are simply interspersed among the domestic, how-to-do-it features and various syndicated human interest columns.

Wherever they appear, these articles and feature items deal with community cultural, social, or educational events that are going to occur in the near future or have recently occurred. They also include informational pieces that the editors feel will be of general interest to readers in the community—a biographical sketch of a local senior citizen, a survey of community health facilities, an interview with a local artist or craftsperson. If these articles do appear in a section of their own, they are usually accompanied by a number of nationally syndicated advice columns or domestic features—an indication of the universality of small-town interests and concerns.

The characteristic features of a community news section include the following:

social calendars of events

social announcements (weddings, engagements, anniversaries, births)

obituaries

detailed information on the time and place of concerts, exhibits, plays

book reviews and theater critiques

gossip columns

club news and program plans

awards and honors received by community members

Before the class undertakes this section survey, locate the community news section and use your discretion in choosing the sorts of articles you feel ought to be focal points in the study. For instance, you may want to disregard obituaries or the listing of honor students in your school, reported at the end of each marking period.

SECTION SURVEY

It may be difficult to isolate community news in a metropolitan daily because its readership is so extensive. Therefore, if the class is subscribing to a metropolitan daily, provide a week's set of newspapers from a smaller city, suburb, or district for a survey of this one section, so that you have about five copies of each day's issue, depending on the size of your class. After you have distributed the papers among the students, have them read every article and feature in the community news section. Ask them to draw a box around each item, underline each headline, and complete a chart like the one following:

Section Inventory Chart

headline	main idea	page / column	writer

This chart can be modified and used with other activities.

When the students have completed this initial survey, have them divide into groups made up of a representative for each day of the week. That is, each group will contain a student who surveyed Monday's paper, another who surveyed Tuesday's, and so on. The students in each group should combine their individual surveys in order to come up with a full week's survey. The full-week survey is important because community news often follows a pattern in which some regular features appear toward the end of the week and others at the beginning. When the groups have prepared their full-week surveys, ask them to complete a group survey using the following questions and procedural guidelines:

Community Section Survey

What is of topical interest to the community? How would you describe the cultural life in your community?

1. Compare the subject matter of articles throughout the week. Come up with several general headings that characterize the material, such as Local Politics, School Social Events, Community Arts, Small Crimes, Local Organizations.
2. Group appropriate headlines under the general headings. If the subject matter of some articles seems unique and the headings are not applicable, make a separate list of these articles. Note their subject matter.

3.   Compute percentages to determine the average distribution of articles within each general subject heading per week. Note any outstanding ratios that might give a clue to which cultural events and interests receive the most attention in your community.

After your group has completed the section survey, discuss your findings. Keep in mind the questions posed at the beginning of the survey. Your data analysis should provide the answers.

FOLLOW-UP FINDINGS

Students can check their perceptions of the cultural activities and interests of people in their community in several ways. These checks may validate or modify the picture they are forming of local culture.

First, they may contact the local editor responsible for community news and ask how he or she acquires the items that appear, and how decisions are made as to which items will be printed and which will not. If possible, have the editor visit the class and discuss this matter at length with students.

Next, students can make copies of the lists of general headings from their surveys; and they can combine and modify them to create one simple, easily understood list. Enough copies of this list should be made so that each student can have five. Then each student will interview five adults and ask them to check the activities on the list that they enjoy reading about. The results of these reader surveys can be compiled for the entire class. Have students compare the reader interest in activities to the frequency with which those activities appear in the newspaper.

As students talk to adults, they may find that many do not read newspapers. If so, you may want to have a work group talk to or write the circulation manager of the newspaper with which the students are working. Ask the group to find out:

the number of households that subscribe to the paper

the number of additional copies sold via newsstands

the number of households in the community

Other information about the readership may be available from the advertising department. In assessing the information obtained from the newspaper staff, students can compute the actual percentage of the households in the community where the newspaper is regularly read. Discuss how this information also contributes to their picture of local culture.

ASSIGNMENT: Cover a Cultural Event

Ask your student reporters to cover a cultural event for a community news section to be assembled by the class. Some students may want to write articles that are simply informative, using an inverted pyramid style. Others may try their hand at features, such as interviews of star performers or local artists, a school talent-scout column, or a descriptive calendar of local cultural events or scheduled school assemblies. Others may choose to write reviews of critiques, developing them in a style similar to the style of an editorial rocket. Therefore, at this time, you may want to broach the subject of *fair comment.*

Fair comment is opinion based on facts that are fairly and accurately stated. Fair comment also means that the writer will carefully support any personal judgment with sound reasons. Locate some specific examples of this in the material the class is studying. You can distinguish fair comment from editorial comment because it does not attempt to persuade the reader by presenting only that information which supports the writer's personal bias. It is a better-balanced form of presentation and evaluation.

Students are now ready to go out into the community and gather the information they will need to write their items. Some may want to interview a YMCA program director to get information about forthcoming events. Others might attend a play given by a local theater group, high school drama class, or junior college players. Students can select activities in which they are already interested or about which they'd like to find out more.

After gathering the information, each student will write his or her item in an appropriate style and format, and compose a headline. Have the class decide on a section heading for their community culture articles. Then assign a staff of editors to plan, lay out, and assemble an over-sized community news section for the class. If there are outstanding contributions, have students submit them on an individual basis to a local newspaper.

SECTION ACTIVITIES

25.   Who Counts?

In reporting about social newsmakers in your community, it is possible that your newspaper practices or upholds certain forms of social discrim-ination. The activities in the following social survey reveal to students how a community's cultural life often defines or underscores its class structure. (If you are teaching in a school system in which issues of class or racial discrimination are particularly sensitive, you will naturally want to use these activities carefully.)

Ask your students to list every name that appears in an item they have boxed in their section survey. Then have them conduct a social survey using the following questions and procedural guidelines:

Social Survey

Do the social and cultural "personalities" in your community belong to an exclusive group? Does your newspaper appear to discriminate according to class, race, sex, occupation, or age?

1.   Review your list of names. Look up each name in the telephone directory and copy the address. Mark the addresses on a street map of your town. Discuss the predominant class and racial features of each area on the map. Compute percentages in order to determine the coverage accorded to the people from each area. Note whether any areas are given an outstandingly large or small percentage of the available space.

2.   Review your list of names. Tally the number of men represented in the cultural community, then tally and compare the number of women. Discuss what kinds of cultural activities attract or promote men and what kinds attract or promote women. Note the number of

auxiliary women's organizations and activities that are specifically designed to promote the activities of male-dominated organizations.

After the class has conducted its survey, discuss the findings in the context of the questions posed at the outset of the survey. Your data analysis should provide the answers.

26. Where Is It All Happening?

Ask your students to list the places mentioned in their boxed articles. Have them mark on the map the locations of the various theaters, halls, religious houses, and other facilities in which community cultural events take place.

Mark in another color the major roads and public transportation routes. Point out that cultural facilities are often located on these routes because they are accessible to and traveled by more people. Have each student make hypothetical plans for getting to a cultural event that he or she is anxious to attend using public transportation. Instruct them to find out the various modes of transportation available, to consult schedules, and to consider all the costs that might be involved in getting to the event.

27. Who Can Afford It?

Some cultural events are free, but others are prohibitively expensive for many people on fixed or low incomes. Ask your students what sort of events they could afford to attend on their present allowances. Then discuss the effort your community makes to present cultural programs and events at an affordable price.

Ask each student to select an event that he or she would like to attend, and plan a budget of the comprehensive costs of attending. Include the following:

admission fee

cost of public transportation (from activity 26)

refreshments

special clothing or equipment (check stores, ads, catalogs)

28. A Scholarly View

If students have already acquired some background in anthropology, they may want to make up an anthropological report describing their community. A typical report might include any of the related information discovered during the study of the community news section as well as the following items:

a physical description of the community, total population, climate, natural resources, landforms, and so forth

a summary of the cultural activities participated in by the inhabitants

comments on the cultural roles identified (activity 25)

6

THE BUSINESS WORLD
Analyzing Today's Economy

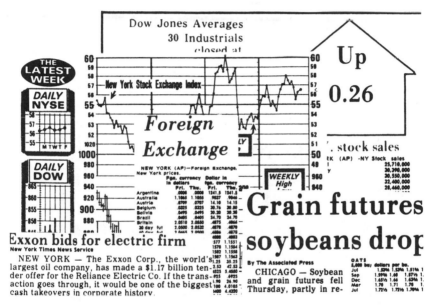

The page or pages devoted to business usually include the stock market reports; a summary of stock trading; information about bonds, currencies, and commodities; and articles offering analysis of, or news about, particular people or organizations in the world of commerce. Other articles may offer the reader advice on investments or information about legislation affecting the economic scene. The business section may also feature syndicated columns by well-known economists and market specialists.

Before the class begins working with this section, you may want to enlist the aid of one or more local stockbrokers. They can provide you with back issues of Standard and Poor's stock analysis books, stock symbol guide sheets, and other useful, informative material. The newspaper under study may also periodically publish general information items such as stock splits, issue rights, or guidelines for reading the stock market tables. Read through the back issues, locate these items, and note them for later use. A banker can also be a helpful resource person, answering students' questions about currencies and interest rates.

The business or financial section of the newspaper is an invaluable source of information for studies in some areas of economics at every level of education. However, many elementary, junior, and high school teachers are unfamiliar with the theory, standard forms of presentation, and terminology used in the business pages. If you count yourself among the uninformed, use the glossary which follows to better acquaint yourself with the commercial language of market investors and traders.

GLOSSARY OF STOCK MARKET TERMS

averages: representative groups of stocks whose quotations are averaged each hour, day, and week to provide a summary of trading and trends

balance of trade: the ratio of a nation's imports to its exports

bear market: a pessimistic decline in stock market prices continuing over a long period of time

bonds: a form of long-term borrowing in which the public or private enterprise in need of capital issues a certificate to the investor that promises to repay the principal at a given date, and to pay interest periodically

bull market: an optimistic rise in stock market prices continuing over a long period of time

capital goods: products which are used in the manufacture of other products and are not themselves directly sold to or used by consumers

compound interest: interest paid on the sum of the original principal and the interest already accrued on that principal, as opposed to interest paid only on the principal itself

consumer goods: products which are sold to and used directly by consumers

currency: coins, paper bills, or notes which are in circulation as a medium of exchange

depression: a period of low economic activity usually marked by a drastic decline in stock market prices, and more generally by an increase in unemployment and lack of productivity

diversify: a practice of investing money in a number of different types of industries and securities

dividend: a fraction of the value of a full share of stock that is distributed periodically to stockholders

futures: commodities purchased at a current rate in anticipation of their future sales value

inflation: a period of economic uncertainty often marked by a rise in stock market prices, and more generally a decrease in the goods-purchasing power of a currency

interest rate: a percentage of a principal paid in addition to the repayment of the principal itself

investment: money put up for securities in anticipation of their greater future market value

liquify: a practice of investors to sell their stock holdings at short notice; selling securities in order to get currency, which is a highly flexible or "liquid" asset

mutual fund: a corporation which simply invests in other corporations, thereby allowing its own smaller investors to have a stake in diversified holdings

over the counter: securities such as bank, insurance, and industrial corporate stocks which are not listed on a stock exchange but are instead traded at brokerage desks

principal: the original amount of money invested

rate of exchange: a ratio expressing the value of one currency based on the value of another currency, or the buying power of one currency compared to another *recession:* a period of reduced economic activity during which stock market prices usually decline

security: shareholdings or bondholdings which represent participation in a business's prosperity and which can be traded on a market

stock: the owned portion of a business which is subdivided into shares represented by stock certificates which are traded on the open market

stock broker: an agent who negotiates the sale and purchase of securities for investors

stock certificate: a paper statement which is evidence of ownership of one or more shares of stock

stock exchange (or *stock market*):   the auction place where listed securities are traded

stock split: a practice of dividing corporate stock and reissuing two or more new shares of lesser value for every original share, thereby increasing the number of overall shares which can be traded and making it possible for more people to own them

trade summary (see *averages*):   a report of average trading for a group of securities

SECTION SURVEY

Distribute a week's worth of business sections so that each student can read thoroughly the consecutive issues' financial pages. After the students have read every article (for the time being disregard the charts and graphs), ask the class to conduct a section survey using the following questions and procedural guidelines:

Business Section Survey

How wide is the topical and regional scope of the articles? To what degree does the newspaper staff contribute to this section? How do front page events influence business coverage?

1.   Assign general headings to those areas of business which receive coverage during the survey period. Such headings might be

Transportation, Insurance, Banking, Agriculture, Capital Goods Industries, Consumer Goods Industries, Natural Resources Development, Construction, and Services. List the articles under their appropriate headings. Some articles may not apply to this study.

2. Code the regional scope of each business article—L for Local, S for State, N for National, and I for International. Code the authorship of each article as well—N for Newspaper Staff Writer, and S for Syndicated Columnist.

3. Compute percentages and ratios to show the distribution of articles according to their content scope, regional scope, and authorship. Draw bar graphs or pie charts to illustrate your findings.

4. Read the news stories on the corresponding front page of your business section. Note any front page articles on events involving or affecting an area of business. If they received concurrent attention in the business section, examine any differences in treatment. Compare your notes with other students in the class who surveyed newspapers on the other consecutive dates.

After the class has conducted its survey, discuss the findings. Keep in mind the questions posed at the beginning of the survey. Your data analysis should provide the answers.

FOLLOW-UP FINDINGS

Using the percentile figures from the section survey, ascertain which area of business received the most coverage during the survey period. Invite one or more people involved in this particular field to visit the class.

In preparation for the visit, have your students read any newspaper articles they can find about the speaker's business. Encourage students to research additional information about the economic status of the business in news magazines and business magazines. Ask each student to prepare several questions for the guest. The questions should delve into the financial structure of the business, its employment practices and labor relations, its stability and performance in the marketplace, the history of its past performance, projections for its future performance, and the effects that fluctuations in the economy and government controls have on its prosperity.

ASSIGNMENT: Contribute to a Community Business Section

Instruct students to come up with a story to contribute to a community business section that the class will assemble. Some may want to re-search the state of an industry such as computer software and report on the use of its updated equipment in local businesses. Others may want to read about affirmative action and labor laws, then interview the manager of a local business to report that business's policies of hiring, firing, and negotiating contracts. A biographical feature on a local business person, the occasion of a new store's grand opening, the closing down of a landmark restaurant or old business establishment, and a photo-essay comparing the downtown commercial center of your community today with the area fifty years ago all constitute com-munity business news.

Encourage students to share their news and feature story develop-ments while they are still in the process of compiling information and following possible "leads." If you encounter would-be Woodward and Bernstein teams, by all means encourage their cooperative efforts. After typewritten stories have been submitted, assign a staff of editors to plan, lay out, and assemble an oversized community business page or section for the class. If there are outstanding contributions, have students submit them on an individual basis to a local newspaper.

SECTION ACTIVITIES

29. Charting the Market

Select a newspaper for this activity that features an index or summary for each day's trading, such as the Dow Jones Averages or Standard and Poor's Index. The summaries usually list five types of securities —industrials, transportations, utilities, stocks, and bonds.

Divide the class into several work groups and assign each group to monitor and chart the progress of one security in the index for a period of a week or more. Duplicate and distribute graphs on which students can record the daily averages for their security group. Explain how to read the indexes. An explanation of the Dow Jones summary is included here for your easy reference. A sample graph for recording the summary figures is found on the following page.

The Dow Jones Averages Index

The Dow Jones Averages measure the average movements of a particular group of well-known stocks on the market. Originally, the Dow Jones Industrial Average was reported as the sum of the quotations of these 30 stocks divided by 30. But numerous stock splits over the years so complicated this figure that today the divisor has been fixed at 2.163 instead of 30. That is why the average is reported to be in the high 800s when in fact each of the surveyed stocks sells for less than $200 a share.

The Dow Jones Averages now include figures for 5 groups of securities—30 industrials, 20 transportations, 15 utilities, 65 stocks, and 20 bonds. It provides an overview of the day's trading by charting the opening price, the high, the low, the closing price, and the net change for each security group. The Dow Jones Averages Index is based on a theory that stocks advance and decline *together* on the market exchange, and therefore show or forecast a business trend.

After students have plotted figures for the entire period, post their graphs on a bulletin board. Engage the class in making a comparative analysis of the progress of the various securities they have charted. Encourage them to observe patterns of fluctuation, stability, and singular performances. Elicit from them intelligent reasons for selecting a particular security or stock group in which to invest.

30.   Bulls and Bears: The Influence of Historic Events on the Market

Ask students to use the library's microfilmed newspapers in order to chart the progress of the stock market during week-long periods in this century in which historic events took place. A sample list of dates appears on page 57.

Stock Activity Graph

Security:_____

Time Period:_____

Net Change:_____

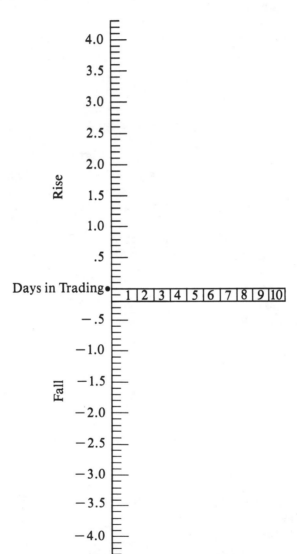

This graph can be modified and used with other activities.

The Week Of

— October 29, 1929 (the stock market crashes)
— October 29, 1934 (the stock market continues to recover)
— December 7, 1941 (attack on Pearl Harbor)
— April 12, 1945 (death of Franklin D. Roosevelt)
— August 6, 1945 (atom bomb dropped on Hiroshima)
— June 25, 1950 (North Korea invades South Korea)
— May 17, 1954 (Brown vs. Board of Education, Topeka)
— December 2, 1954 (Senate resolution condemning Joseph R. McCarthy)
— September 9, 1957 (Civil Rights Act)
— October 5, 1957 (Russians launch Sputnik, first orbiting satellite)
— January 3, 1959 (Alaska becomes a state)
— February 20, 1962 (John Glenn orbits the earth)
— October 22, 1962 (Cuban missile crisis)
— November 22, 1963 (assassination of John F. Kennedy)
— August 11, 1966 (Watts race riots)
— April 30, 1970 (U.S. escalates war in Cambodia)
— May 4, 1970 (Kent State killings)
— August 9, 1974 (Richard M. Nixon's resignation)

Have students observe which events caused a bull market (an optimistic rise in stock market prices) and a bear market (a pessimistic decline in stock market prices). Direct their attention to the pattern of market performance during war periods.

31. Investing in the Stock Market

Announce to your class that a pretend beneficiary has bequeathed each student $1,000 to invest in the stock market. Students must invest in stocks that they believe—after some research—will give them the greatest return on their investment by the end of the semester or newspaper unit.

In preparation, encourage students to research the trends and recent progress of the stocks in which they would like to invest. They should consult any resource materials made available to the class by local stockbrokers, as well as the business sections of their newspapers and articles from other news and business magazines. Discourage them from capriciousness and thoughtless speculation.

Have each student write up a buy order when he or she has chosen up to a maximum of five stocks in which to invest. Assign a student broker to record the sale price on the initial day of "purchase." During the investment period, students can be permitted to liquify, diversify, or sell their stocks in order to buy others. Each transaction must be recorded by the broker. At the end of the investment period, have each student calculate his or her profit or loss. More mature students can also compute the broker's fees on these transactions and keep track of any dividends paid during the period.

You may allow more able students to reserve the opinion to diversify and continue trading if they can effectively monitor their market investments over the assigned period without confusion. Younger students should be permitted to buy only one stock and required to hold onto their original investments.

32. A Dollar Here, A Dollar There

International currency values are important indications of the current strength of various nations' economies in the world-trade market. Our currency can be converted according to the present rate of exchange, and the amount of foreign currency obtained can be compared to the amount we would have received at other times in the past. If the dollar buys less foreign currency today, point out that this means it is inflated, reflecting a weakness in the national economy. If the dollar is worth more, this indicates a strengthened national economy or a weakened international economy.

Write the current exchange rates on the board and ask students to compute what the dollar is worth today in yen, marks, pounds sterling, and so on. Then have each student choose a different year in the past from among the years for which newspapers are available on microfilm. Ask them to complete the following steps:

1.   Locate the date corresponding to today for the year you have chosen or the date of the business day closest to it. Remember, there is no trading on Sundays and no report in Monday issues.
2.   Copy dollar exchange information and use it to compute the dollar's value on that past date in the various international currencies.
3.   Write the date and information on the board.

This done, ask the students to analyze the information. To guide the analysis, ask:

When was the dollar worth more? Less?

What does this mean in terms of today's economy?

What kind of events can cause a significant rise or decline of the dollar?

Discuss the effects of decontrol, embargoes, announced depletions of commodities such as gold, investment regulations, surpluses, and other economic policy changes and indicators on the value of the dollar in international trade.

33. Balancing Trade

Ask students to clip all the articles they can find that relate to the balance of trade, trade agreements with other nations, trade restrictions or controls, and so forth. They may use the issues from the survey period and other newspapers as well. Be sure that each clipped article is mounted on a sheet of paper with the date of the issue and name of the newspaper clearly written on the paper. Have the students read these articles, keeping in mind the following questions:

With which country or countries does the United States trade the most?

What central topics or issues are involved?

If you were a negotiator, how would you handle trade with another country based on your country's best interests and trade relations with that other country?

Students can respond to this last question by working up impromptu sketches based on information they have from this study, with one or two people representing the other nation and one or two as trade negotiators from the U.S. Encourage students to simulate such negotiations between the U.S. and an oil-producing nation (Saudi Arabia or Mexico), and the U.S. and China (a potentially large import/export market).

34. More Trading

Stocks are not the only items traded nationally. Students will also read reports of trading on the commodity markets including copper, silver, and gold futures; investment funds; stock options; treasury notes; livestock; grain; and others. The newspaper rarely contains any explanatory material about these kinds of trading; usually only a report is given. If students want to learn more about trading in any of these areas, arrange for a classroom visit from a broker or another resource person.

35.   Keeping Up with Inflation

Throughout this newspaper study, students will notice articles about the current inflation rates. Sometimes this information makes the front page news; at other times it is covered in the business section. Such information is usually released once a month for the month before. There may also be articles that compare the current month's inflation rate with the overall rate for the preceeding year or recent years. Post the most recent figures available.

Inform your students that they have each been given $1,000 to deposit in the bank. Ask them to find out the current interest rate for a day-of-deposit/day-of-withdrawal savings account which is compounded daily at a bank in town. Have them compare that figure to the current inflation rate. Are they keeping up with inflation by saving their money in the bank? If not, ask them to compute the value they are losing over a year on the $1,000 deposit.

7

SPORTS SCENE
Scouting the Action

Horton Automatics 6, Deputies 4
B.D. Holt 24, Mack Sales 16
AMOCO 22, A.T.C. 2
Kiwanis Field
CP&L 7, Memorial Medical 0, forfeit
Firefighters 3, Cooper's Alley 2
Seagulls 10, Scarlet Knights 7
Coca-Cola 12, Angels 5
Price Field
Exxon Tigerettes 11, Oasis 5
All-State Wreckers 26, Coastal States 12

Okay Meats 9, CCPC 9
Huff's Food Town #1 14, Budd Electric 11

World 600

CHARLOTTE, N.C. — The qual-

Major League

AMERICAN LEAGUE
EAST

	W	L	Pct.	GB
Baltimore	28	14	.667	—
Boston	25	16	.610	2½
Milwaukee	25	20	.556	4½
New York	22	18	.550	5

Sports in Brief

Major League Boxscores

National

	ab	r	h	bi		ab	r	h	bi
HOUSTON					**SAN DIEGO**				
Puhl rf	4	0	1	1	Richrds df	4	1	0	0
CRenlds ss	3	0	0	0	Bevacq 3b	4	0	0	0
Cedeno cf	4	0	0	0	BEvans 3b	0	0	0	0
JCruz lf	3	0	1	0	Briggs lf	3	0	1	1
Cabell 3b	4	0	0	0	Winfield rf	4	0	1	0
Watson 1b	3	0	0	0	Tenace c	4	0	1	0
Ashby c	3	0	1	0	Almon ss	0	0	0	0
Sexton pr	0	0	0	0	Hargrv 1b	4	0	1	0
Bochy c	1	0	0	0	FGnzlz 2b	4	1	1	1
Landsty 2b	4	0	1	0	OSmith ss	3	0	0	0
Williams p	2	0	0	0	Kendall c	1	0	1	0
Walling ph	1	1	1	0	Perry p	3	0	0	0
Sambito p	0	0	0	0	DRnlds ph	1	0	0	0
					Fingers p	0	0	0	0
Total	32	1	5	1	**Total**	35	2	6	2

Houston   000 000 000 0—1
San Diego   010 000 000 1—2

E—Hornia 9.

Ongais says he feels fine

Race driver **Danny Ongais**, insisting that he feels fine, complained that "bureaucracy" is preventing him from making a qualification attempt for the

ifiers for Sunday's $363,0
stock car race at the 1.5
lotte Motor Speedway,
average speed.
1. Neil Bonnett, 160.125
cury
2. Richard Petty, 159.82
3. Darrell Waltrip, 159.
let
4. Benny Parsons, 159.
Chevrolet
5. Cale Yarborough, 1!
mobile
6. Donnie Allison, 158
Chevrolet
7. Bobby Allison, 158.4(
8. Buddy Baker, 158.39(
9. Bill Elliott, 158.092, /
10. Ricky Rudd, 157.741,
11. Ron Hutcherson, 157
12. Joe Millikan, 157.502
*13. Coo Coo Marlin, 157.
let
14. Dave Marcis, 157.24
15. Terry Labonte, 157.2
16. Dale Earnhardt, 160.
let
17. Connie Saylor, 159.6
bile
18. Harry Gant, 158.339,
19. Bobby Fisher, 157.90
cury
21. Al Holbert, 156.931, (
22. Glenn Jarrett, 156.47
23. Tighe Scott, 156.399,
24. Richard Childress,
mobile
25. Dick Brooks, 156.092.
26. Skip Manning, 155.62
27. James Hylton, 155.51
28. Grant Adcox, 155.23
29. Bobby Wawak, 155.0(
30. Travis Tiller, 154.85
31. John Kennedy, 154.8
32. Lennie Pond, Chev
33. J.D. McDuffie, Chev

A wide range of articles relating to most sports can be found in the section of the newspaper most popularly known as the sports pages. Sometimes the sports pages are printed on colored paper and are listed under such section heads as "The Sporting Green" or "The World of Sports."

Articles in the sports pages cover news updates and factual information about a seasonal spectator game or series, a current tournament, or other scheduled sports event. Such reports may include scores, averages, and other statistical information that fans might want to study as well as a description of the action. Often sports writers employ colorful sports jargon, which is familiar to avid sports fans.

The sports pages also include human interest items. These features focus on various sports personalities, offering biographical sketches and a behind-the-scenes view of managerial activities within leagues and contract negotiations. In addition to material dealing with spectator sports, some papers regularly run items about other forms of physical recreation in which the reader might participate. Such articles would include angler's information pieces, seasonal hunting guides, how-to or advice features on water sports, skiing, jogging and exercising, pointers for one-on-one court games, or recommendations for trail hikes and bicycle tours.

In short, the sports section has a little bit of everything. It contains some straight news stories, occasional editorial remarks by the section editor, regular sports commentary, human interest features, and a lot of statistics—all of which relate to sports.

SECTION SURVEY

Students will now be several weeks into their study of the newspaper. There should be an accumulation of at least thirty consecutive issues of a daily paper for class use. For this section survey, provide each student with a different day's issue of the same paper. Ask students to conduct an independent survey using the following questions and procedural guidelines:

Sports Section Survey

Which sports receive the most extensive coverage? What level of competition—college, amateur, professional, or Olympic (If applicable)—receives the most coverage? Can you speculate on the distribution of articles during other seasons?

1.   Tally the number of articles devoted to each sport in your issue. Add the total number of column inches devoted to coverage of each

sport. Compute percentages to determine the extent of coverage for each sport in the day's issue. Note any outstanding ratios. Note which sports are currently in season.

2. Tally the number of articles featuring sports at each level of competition. Add the total number of column inches devoted to each level of competition. Compute percentages to determine the extent of coverage for each level of competition in the day's issue. Note any outstanding ratios. (If you are using a small community paper, include major and minor community leagues and high school competition as levels.)

3. Combine your findings with the findings of the other students in your class. Compute new percentages and note overall patterns.

After everyone in the class has completed the survey, compare and discuss your findings. Keep in mind the questions posed at the beginning of the survey. Your data analysis should provide the answers.

FOLLOW-UP FINDINGS

Students should be encouraged to validate their statistical findings from the section survey. Here are several comparative methods that can be used in class. Choose those that are appropriate and can be worked into your schedule.

Invite a sports writer from the staff of the newspaper to visit the class and talk about how stories are chosen for the sports pages. Encourage students to take notes and use this person's perspective to modify the generalizations they made in their section survey.

Students can also monitor the TV news for sports coverage. Ask them to conduct a similar survey for each monitored broadcast. The notation of minutes and seconds used will replace column inches to quantify coverage. The results of this survey can be compared with survey results for the sports sections of the newspaper on corresponding days.

If students have been working with a local community paper thus far, arrange for delivery of several days' sports sections from a metropolitan daily. If students have been working with a metropolitan daily, arrange for delivery of several days' newspapers from a smaller city. Ask students to work in groups, and have each group conduct a section survey for the new paper. Complete an analysis of the coverage. Discuss the difference between sports coverage in a metropolitan daily and corresponding coverage in a small-city newspaper. Does the small-city newspaper focus primarily on local sports events, or does it also cover, say, the activities of a major team in a nearby metropolitan area?

ASSIGNMENT: Cover a Sports Event

Assign your students a sports story for a classroom issue of sports pages. Permit them to cover a live sports event or to interview a star athlete, coach, or trainer, either at school or from the local community. Make each student responsible for a well-documented, descriptive news story or feature written in an appropriate journalistic format. If your students are agreeable, assign the same proportion of students to cover a sport as coverage is given to that sport in the sports section of the newspaper under current study. (See the Section Survey.)

Encourage students to go over any information about which they feel unsure, verify any statistics, and check the final draft of their interviews with the persons featured in the interviews. Encourage them to use effective jargon and vivid verbs to make their description of the action exciting and fast-paced.

Assign a staff of editors to plan, lay out, and assemble an oversized sports section using the class's contributions. If there are outstanding contributions, encourage students to submit them on an individual basis to the school or local newspaper. If your study of the newspaper encompasses more than one sports season, repeat the assignment so that students can reapply their sports writing skills to another sports activity.

SECTION ACTIVITIES

36. Sports Talk

Many sports writers use a special language or jargon that is familiar to fans and professionals in the field, but foreign to occasional readers. Ask your students to reread articles in the sports section looking out for any examples of sports jargon. The following words may appear on their lists:

ace	bogie
dunk	dribble
pigskin	safety
hit and run	bullpen
sink	wipe out
birdie	blitz

Compare lists in class. Elicit from your most sports-knowledgeable students the popular definitions of the listed words. Ask the students to enter the words and the accompanying definitions on individual index cards, and alphabetize the entries in a file box provided by you. If students are particularly intrigued by the use of jargon, extend your study of subject-specific language to such fields as music, radio communications (citizens' band, military), youth culture (past and present), and newspaper publishing in general. Appoint a staff of editors to compile the alphabetized index cards into a supplement to the classroom dictionary.

37. Retrospect in Sports

Have your students conduct a comparative survey for the current season's sports pages during a year in recent but not too recent history. First, as a class, select one particular day in the season to survey (the date of April 15 was selected for the illustration on page 67). Then request that each student select a different year—you might want to assign spans of decades or five-year periods—for which an issue of the newspaper is available on microfilm in the library. Have each student note which sport dominated the news and list all others which received lesser coverage on the prescribed day during the year the student has chosen.

Compare survey findings in class. Then prepare a time-line display of sports coverage for the current season. Have students design large pictures or symbols to designate the dominant sports for each year in the survey. Then have them design smaller pictures to designate the sports which received less coverage during each time period. Arrange the pictures in a montage under the appropriate dates on the time-line.

An interesting variation of this activity would be to conduct a comparative survey and study of the current season's most widely covered sports in other countries. You would need to provide foreign newspapers—preferably English-language papers from such countries and territories as England, Canada, Australia, Ireland, Scotland, Wales, New Zealand, Hong Kong, the British West Indies, and South Africa.

38.   What Are the Odds?

If horseracing information is carried in your paper, ask students to locate all the items that relate to one track. They will probably find one chart that gives the names of the horses entered in each race, the names of the jockeys, other general information, and the odds. A second item usually found near the handicap chart is a list of selections made for each race by several people on the sports staff. Both of these items relate to the races that will be run that day. The students may also find a third schedule or chart showing the outcomes of the races run the previous day—which horse won, what was paid, and so forth.

If possible arrange for a visit by someone familiar with horseracing to find out more about how these charts are prepared. Using the current incoming issues, students can study the charts and selection lists relating to the races scheduled for that day and make their choices. When the results are printed in the following day's paper, the students can see how many winners they picked. Ask students to compute how much money they would have won or lost if they had bought a $2.00 (or minimum amount) ticket for each of their selections.

39.   Series Standings

Throughout most of the year, one or more professional leagues will be in competition. The sports section will publish the standings of all the teams in the league, updated after each game. Ask your students to look at the series standings for the current season's spectator sport. Have each student pick a team to follow for the remainder of the season. If there are not enough teams to go around, move to a second league or to another sport.

Retrospect in Sports
Spring Sports Coverage

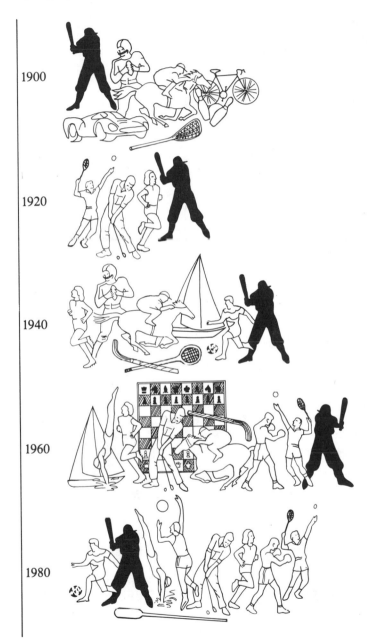

1900

1920

1940

1960

1980

Supply the following chart on which students can record the wins and losses of their teams:

Team Standings Chart

Team:_____

Date	Wins	Losses	Percentage	Games Behind

Students should continue to record this information daily. In order to have a complete season's chart, have them also work backwards, recording back-dated information from earlier issues of the paper until they come to the first date on which the standings were published for the teams during the current season. When the chart is complete, ask students to write a paragraph each summarizing their teams' win records for the season.

40.   Most Valuable Player

Some students may prefer to follow a particular player rather than a team. Have these students choose one athlete and record his or her playing statistics on the chart found on page 69.

As the season closes, ask those students who charted player statistics to compare the records of the athletes and write a paragraph summarizing the seasonal performance of their players. Then have the students vote on the "Most Valuable Player" among those under study, based on the players' seasonal records.

Player Statistics Chart

Player:_____

Sport:_____

Position:_____

Date	At Bat	Hits	Home Runs	Runs Batted In	Average

Use appropriate statistical headings for various sports and positions.

41. Men Only?

In reading some sports sections, the reader might come away with the idea that the section is for men only. Have your students decide if this is the case with the papers they are studying. Have them conduct a week's survey of the sports section using the following procedural guidelines:

1. Over a period of a week, measure the number of column inches devoted to the activities of women in sports.
2. Measure the total number of column inches devoted to all sports in the survey period.
3. Compute the percentage of coverage devoted to women in sports.

Discuss your findings. Ask your students to note the kinds of sports in which women are most involved. Some students may want to talk with local sports people in order to prepare a schedule of games or events involving women's or girls' teams at the high school and college levels. Other students can report on professional women's sports events in the area.

8

NEWSPAPER FEATURES
Exploring Diverse Interests

Current Best Sellers

New York Times News Service

FICTION
1. THE MATARESE CIRCLE, Robert ...

...OOD AS GOLD, Joseph Heller.
...ANTA YO, Ruth Beebe Hill.
...AR AND REMEMBRANCE, Her...

common cents
By KATE MacQUEEN
Better to use a plung-
er on a stopped-up drain
before you pour in a
strong drain cleaner.
the cleaner doesn't open
the drain and you try the
plunger, water in the
sink holds the water
cleaner. If the water
splashes onto your skin
when using the plunger,
you could suffer a skin
burn. Chronicle Features

...GB, Len Deighton.
...SAPEAKE, James A. Michener.
...RLOAD, Arthur Hailey.
...TORIES OF JOHN CHEEVER

... STORY, Peter Straub.
...HIRD WORLD WAR: AUG
... John Hackett and other top-
...erals and advisors.
GENERAL
...MPLETE SCARSDAL
...nan Tarnower, M.D. a
...RONX ZOO, Sparky Lyle
...ilcock.
3. HOW TO PROSPER DURING T

Set out mums

CANCER (June 21-July 22): Accen.
new approach to long-standing problem.
Accept challenge — you are due to suc.
ceed. Leo ...
...persons play key
...ich, in recent past
...rful. Light will re

22): Intuition, ex-
could come into
Cancer message.
...ibility. Do plenty
...ting." Check fi-
ons.

... 22): Avoid di-
...r for time, play
focuses on legal
...be permanent,
...ini, Sagittarius
full rein to in-

Korean art display
San Francisco's Asian Art Museum in Gold
en Gate Park is the site of a major exhibi
tion this summer entitled, "5,000 Y
Korean Art." The 345
which will be di...
cludes th...

Robin Adams Sloan

Many articles printed in newspapers are of general and human interest, rather than of newsworthy importance. The information included in this feature material is not unlike the information in a typical home and family magazine. The subject matter is seasonal but not date-specific, so that it is relevant for a longer period than news material. From a functional standpoint, these kinds of articles can be collected or written at any time and used to fill up the newspaper pages as needed. In fact, some features are referred to as "fillers."

Photographs are important in features. News stories sometimes have accompanying photos, but features almost always have photos. Often a feature photo will be on the front page and the reader will be given an inside page reference for the story. Sometimes a feature photo will only have a caption; the story will be told by the photo.

Some feature material is used in every edition on any page that is short of copy, but the best of it is often reserved for a weekly magazine section. This usually accompanies the Sunday edition of the paper, although some publishers prefer to distribute it with Saturday's paper. The magazine section often has a four-color picture on the cover and is assembled as a self-contained magazine rather than as a folded newspaper section.

Magazine-type features include such items as a once-a-week food and recipe section, a seasonal fashion preview, a home decorating supplement, and an interview with a celebrity or an artistic or literary personality. Generally, these features deal with matters of domestic interest—home management, handicrafts, leisure, gardens, health, travel, and the family. (If you're thinking that some of these features might overlap with those in the community news section, you're absolutely right.)

The style varies. Some features are written in a news format, using the inverted pyramid structure. Others, such as how-to-do-it pieces, are expository. The feature writer gives directions and steps in a clear sequence. How-to features include recipes, gardening tips, and descriptions of handicrafts. Biographical features focusing on people who have made significant domestic or artistic contributions are frequently written in an interview format or in a nicely developed, informal prose. Articles that explore the history of tourist attractions or the history and current activities of a group of people would be written in the same descriptive manner.

Magazine editors may select from a broad range of material and may expand the sphere of subject matter to reflect the interests of their readership. This section often includes poems, photo-journalistic essays, and other essays. These creative pieces provide a style of writing that contrasts with the reportorial matter-of-factness of the rest of the paper.

Any or all of these kinds of articles may be written by staff writers. However, some will probably come as news releases from food processors and others in industries that sell home or garden products. The editors will also include syndicated articles and advice columns on personal interest subjects such as health and psychology.

SECTION SURVEY

Provide students with a week's worth of magazine sections, giving one section to each student. (Several students will be using issues of the same date.) If there is no regular magazine section, distribute the entire paper and have students focus on the areas where feature material seems to be clustered. After the students have identified and read every feature article, ask them to conduct a section survey using the following questions and procedural guidelines:

Magazine Section Survey

What is the topical distribution of feature articles? To what extent does the newspaper staff contribute to the magazine section? What writing styles characterize feature stories and fillers? To what extent does the paper use feature material for filler?

1.   List feature articles under topical headings such as Domestic (home and family), Health, Crafts, Travel, History, Famous Personalities, and Etiquette. Measure the column inches of coverage devoted to each and compute percentages. Draw a pie chart to graph comparisons.

2.   List feature articles under authorship headings such as Staff Writer, Syndicated Columnist, Local Contributor, and Commercial Contributor. Tally the number of articles under each heading and compute percentages.

3.   List feature articles under stylistic headings such as Reportorial, Editorial, Informal Prose, Interview Format, Question-and-Answer, Expository, and Creative (includes prose, poetry, and art). Tally the number of articles under each heading. Note the style of any features that do not fall into these general categories.

4.   Look through the entire issue of the newspaper and count the number of features used in other sections to fill up leftover space.

5.   Compare your findings with those of students who surveyed the other issues of the paper. Note any outstanding patterns and discrepancies. If there is a date on which there are conspicuously few features, check the paper once again to see if a sudden newsbreak or news story caused an imbalance of news/feature coverage for that day.

After all the students have completed the survey, compare and discuss the findings. Keep in mind the questions posed at the beginning of the survey. Your data analysis should provide the answers.

FOLLOW-UP FINDINGS

Ask your students to conduct a survey of feature material included in several nationally distributed magazines. Make available a large selection of publications representing a variety of types—news magazines, domestic magazines, sports magazines, creative writing and arts magazines, lifestyle magazines, trade magazines, and entertainment magazines. Assign each student at least one magazine to read thoroughly. Ask them to make the following observations:

What is the interest focus of the magazine? Compared to the newspaper, is it news- or feature-oriented?

How many articles in the magazine are date-specific, that is, they could not be included in an earlier or later issue without losing their relevance?

How many articles are not date-specific?

Have students compare their observations about the different interest focuses of magazines. Encourage them to make generalizations about the corresponding balance of news and feature coverage in news- and feature-oriented magazines.

ASSIGNMENT: Write a How-To Feature

Ask your students to list their skills or hobbies or processes with which they are very familiar. From this list have each select a topic on which he or she feels knowledgeable and write a how-to article. Although the how-to article is only one of the formats used for magazine articles, it does offer students an opportunity to write in an expository style.

Explain to your students that a how-to article has the following three-part structure:

1. The *lead-in* introduces the topic.
2. The *steps* explain the process in an orderly sequence.
3. The *conclusion* describes the finished item or summarizes the process.

Ask students to use the Who? Chart in order to narrow down their topics and to make them more specific and interesting. In this way "Starting a Campfire" might become "One Way to Get a Campfire Going in the Rain" or "How to Start a Campfire with One Match." In doing this, the student will be answering the What? and either the How? or the When? parts of the Who? Chart. Satisfying two or three items of the chart will usually limit a topic conveniently. Remind the students to be sure to cover the other chart items in the first few sentences of the lead-in. Then they can list the steps numerically and describe the finished item.

When the students have completed a first draft of their articles, suggest that they exchange with a partner to test one another's directions for accuracy and clarity. Any omissions should be pointed out to the writer by the partner. Next have students prepare final drafts of their articles with any necessary modifications, compose catchy headlines, and post their finished articles on a board display. Discourage the use of illustrations and diagrams. Insist that precise and clear prose serve as the only method of demonstration.

Before the students begin writing their how-to articles, you may want to have them try this step-by-step procedure: "How to Make a Press Operator's Hat." This hat was worn by printers operating presses in this country during the eighteenth century to protect their hair from ink, grease, oil, and paper lint. Either read these directions to the class or distribute copies.

1. Take a four-page sheet of your daily newspaper. Fold it in half and lay it down in front of you with the fold at the top.
2. Determine the vertical centerline and fold the top left corner down to it.
3. Fold the top right corner down to the centerline.
4. Fold the lower edge of the top sheet up to the base of the triangle and crease.
5. Again fold this edge up to form the hatband. Turn hat over.

6.   Fold the right edge to a point about ½ inch past the centerline. This will give you a hat that fits an average-size head. For a larger size fold the edge to about ¼ inch past the centerline. Fold the left side in the same manner to the centerline.

7.   Fold the lower right and left corners up to the bottom of the hatband.

8.   Fold the lower flap up over hatband, then turn the top edge of this flap toward the hat and tuck it down into the hatband.

9.   Fold the peak down to the bottom of the hatband and tuck it under the band. (It helps to tape the peak in place).

10. Pick up the hat and open it, flattening out the top. Fold the two resulting peaks down to the bottom of the hat, crease to hold the fold, and tuck tips into the band. Now you have a press operator's hat.

When your students have tried these directions, you may want to ask:

Are there any directions you would add to this list?

Are there any that could be left out?

What other changes would you make based on your own experience?

Students may want to try writing their own version of "How to Make a Press Operator's Hat," or write directions (words only allowed) for other complex processes. Any such written directions should be tested on several readers.

SECTION ACTIVITIES

42.   Some Leg Work

Select a community facility that meets the following requirements: activities are taking place, information of a general nature is available, and the staff is accessible. This might be a community nature center, the main library, a neighborhood swimming pool, or a similar place. Arrange a field trip. Be sure the staff members are available to demonstrate what they do and are willing to be interviewed by students.

Before the day of the visit, ask each student to decide which kind of article he or she would like to write—a general information news story, a how-to article, a human interest biography, or something else in keeping with magazine-type feature material.

Once the students have decided which format or structure they will use, they can list the kinds of information they will need to get from the field trip. During the class visit, students will be responsible for getting the information they need. Some may take photographs or make drawings to accompany their writing. Following the field trip, students will compose their articles.

43.   All Ticketed Passengers!

Provide each student with the travel section of a newspaper. Travel information may appear only in the Sunday edition, or it may be a regular feature on a particular weekday. Instruct students to read through the section and think about the resorts and cities they would most like to visit. After each student has made a decision, have him or her pinpoint the place on a notebook-size copy of a world map that you have handed out, then plan a detailed itinerary for a trip.

Sometimes information about plane schedules, cruise ship sailings, and chartered bus tours is printed in the section ads. Ask your students to use this information as they plan their itinerary and costs using the following outline:

A. *Flight Plans*

1.   When does your flight depart?
2.   From where does your flight depart?
3.   Are there any stopovers or changeovers?
4.   When and where does your flight arrive?
5.   Will you need additional transportation to your final destination? Or while you are there?
6.   When does your flight depart for the return trip?
7.   When and where does your return flight arrive?
8.   What is the cost of a round-trip ticket? If you require additional ground transportation, how much will that add to your transportation costs?

B. *Land Package*

1.   What accommodations are available?
2.   Is there a meal plan at the place where you will stay?
3.   How much will your bed and board cost?

C. *Sightseeing and Recreation*

1. What is there to do?
2. What is there to see?
3. What kind of clothing is appropriate for the climate and for your activities?
4. What additional costs will you incur in your sightseeing, recreation, and any necessary clothing purchases?

D. *What Are Your Total Costs?*

Generally students will be unable to answer all these questions working only with the travel section of the newspaper. To help them complete their travel plans, interview several local travel agents and select one who is interested in talking with students. Arrange to have the class visit the agent's office in small groups. Give the agent a specific list of questions for which the students will want answers. The business of making travel arrangements is complex these days—there are dozens of airline schedules to consider, for example—and it is not the intent of this activity to explore every possibility. It can be irritating to travel agents if students come in individually and take up a lot of time asking for this kind of detailed planning for a hypothetical trip. However, by allowing an agent to respond to very specific questions with a group of students, you can offer the students the experience of planning a trip and still keep peace with the travel bureaus of your community.

44. Dear Doctor

Question-and-answer columns about health and articles concerning exercise, diet, relaxation techniques, and so forth are included in the magazine section of the newspaper. If such a column is a regular feature in your newspaper, ask students to locate and read it. Have them note the main idea of each reader question and discuss the following:

What area of the body concerned the greatest number of people?

For what age group do you think this column was planned?

Which words best characterize the doctor's responses? (Elicit "professional," "informative," "sympathetic," "patronizing.")

Ask your students to locate an edition of their newspaper for approximately the same date at least fifty years previously. Have them apply the same questions to a medical column that appeared then. Discuss whether or not the focus of medicine has changed, and whether there were any apparent taboos (note euphemisms). Encourage students to talk about the state of the art of medicine today compared with their grandparents' day.

45. Class Cookbook

Encourage your students to try out some of the recipes they find in the magazine or feature section of the newspaper and report on (or better yet, bring in) their successes to the class. In preparation for their homework, read through several recipes in class, expanding the abbreviations and identifying unknown ingredients. Underscore important sequences such as preheating the oven, sifting before mixing, and premeasuring ingredients. Impress on your students that short cuts are generally not advisable in cooking.

If students are not particularly enthusiastic about experimenting with the newspaper recipes, insist that they each try out a family recipe and bring the results to class. Then ask them to write out the recipe in a clear, expository style, using the format that they have come to recognize as characteristic of a recipe. Compile all their contributions and assemble them in a class cookbook. If possible, reproduce enough copies for each student to take home.

9

DISPLAY ADVERTISING
Questioning the Sponsors

Display advertising plays a major role in the publication of the daily newspaper. The revenue collected from advertising sponsors contributes heavily to the financial support of the paper. Display ads fill up a great deal of space and contain much varied information. For the most part, they promote consumer products and services with text and illustrations. Occasionally political candidates or interest groups invest in display advertising to publicize their campaigns and causes.

The advertising salespeople for a newspaper solicit ads from local businesses and from national accounts. It is common practice for a business to enter into a contract with a newspaper to buy a certain number of inches of ad space over a year and then to use that space whenever needed. Display ads contracted for in this way provide the paper with steady income, and guarantee the business person ad space even during seasons when that space is at a premium.

Many retail businesses plan their advertisements weeks and even months in advance. Display ads are usually drawn up and delivered to the newspaper a week or more before the date on which they appear. The advertiser may request that the ad be placed in a particular section, but the production department has the final word on an ad's location. Because the ads are available to the paper several days in advance, they are usually arranged on the pages at that time, and the pages are assembled into sections. The space left over is then filled with news items and other material that becomes available as the deadline for the edition approaches.

Large national ads—for example, those run by the airlines—may be scheduled further in advance than local retail ads. Also, cigarette, liquor, and TV program ad campaigns are often generated in national advertising agencies and may be part of long-range planning.

Local business sponsorship of a national product is generally found in what is called the *co-op ad,* which features a nationally distributed product and lists the local merchants who carry it. The cost of the co-op ad is divided among the local merchants and the national producer of the product.

There is academic as well as practical value in making a study of the display advertising found in the daily newspaper. The amount of space devoted to it, the price and predominance of certain kinds of merchandise (household products and budget items versus services and luxury items), and the stylistic presentation of the advertising offer additional sociological insights into the readership of the newspaper.

SECTION SURVEY

Have the class survey a week's worth of complete current newspaper editions. If there are not enough issues, divide students into cooperative work groups. Have the class as a whole conduct a survey of the display advertising in the week's consecutive issues using the following questions and procedural guidelines:

Display Advertising Survey

What sort of product or service receives the most coverage over the week? How much space on the average per day is devoted to display advertising? Are there any observable patterns in coverage over the week? How do advertisers use language and visual presentation to persuade people to buy?

1. List the items and services promoted in display advertising over the week under general headings such as Food, Furniture, Travel Transportation, General Merchandise, Financing, or Banking. First measure the column inches devoted to all display ads, then measure the column inches devoted to each heading and compute percentages. Draw a pie chart to graph comparisons.

2. By now you should have a working figure for the number of column inches per page for your newspaper. Multiply this number by the cumulative number of pages of the one week's issues in order to find the number of column inches of newsprint for the week. Divide this number into the number of column inches devoted to display ads for the week (see step 1) in order to ascertain the percentage of space devoted to display advertising during the week.

3. Review your general headings. Note whether the ads under a particular heading happen to appear during a certain part of the week, or on a particular day, or in any other observable pattern. Include space arrangement in your considerations.

4. Note which advertisements attract your eye. Describe the visual devices used, such as a large and bold typeface, detailed illustrations, and other graphics.

5. Note which advertising copy is most persuasive. Describe the kind of language used to persuade people to buy. Discuss the ways in which ads "come on."

After the survey has been completed, discuss the findings. Keep in mind the questions posed at the beginning of the survey. Your data analysis should provide the answers.

FOLLOW-UP FINDINGS

Students can add to their generalized analysis of display advertising by surveying ads in other newspapers and asking comparative questions. Provide one or two editions from several other newspapers issued during the same week as the survey period. Students can work in small groups, each group analyzing one edition by following the same procedures used in the section survey. Pose these additional questions:

Which paper had the largest total space devoted to advertisements?

In different newspapers issued on the same day, are similar products advertised? If not, in what ways are the products different?

Are the words used in ads similar from paper to paper? Are there any differences?

Are there any differences in illustrations or graphics?

ASSIGNMENT: Design and Write a Display Ad

Ask your students to think of an item they own, would like to own, or happen to know a good deal about; then have them design and write copy for a display ad for the item. If some students are unable to make a choice, bring in several copies of household or sporting goods catalogs and suggest that they choose from among the featured items.

Have students review the samples of persuasive language culled from display ads in the section survey. Encourage them to adapt appropriate words and phrases to the copy for their own ads. Remind them, however, to consider the person who might buy their particular item or product and how best to appeal to that kind of person.

Have students draft some rough copy for their ads. As they revise the copy and are better able to judge how much space it will take up, they should also be thinking about how they will illustrate the ad, where the illustration will be positioned, what size the finished ad will be, and what styles of type will be used. (Booklets showing examples of common display typefaces are available from printers at little or no cost.)

To complete their ads, students will need a sheet of white art paper, a straight edge, and a felt pen. Activity steps:

1. Mark the horizontal and vertical dimensions of the ad.

2. Place the illustration, if any, in position and secure with glue. Illustrations may be drawn by hand, traced, clipped from other sources, and so forth.

3. Neatly write or type the copy and position it attractively in the space. (Some students may want to try using transfer lettering from an art-supply store. It is easy to work with and produces a professional effect.)

Display all the completed ads. Encourage your students to discuss what they discovered about the concept and design—and the manipulative intent—of display ads that they were not aware of before. Find out what the standard charge is for display space in your newspaper, and ask each student to calculate the cost of running his or her ad.

SECTION ACTIVITIES

46. Shopping Spree

Announce that each student has been budgeted an imaginary $500 to go on a shopping spree. The only restriction is that he or she may only "buy" items that have been advertised in one edition of the newspaper.

Ask your students to draw up a comprehensive shopping list for themselves, specifying the items they plan to buy, the names of the stores, the locations of the stores, and the prices of the items. If sales tax is applicable in the area, they must figure this tax and include it in the total cost. This total must not exceed $500.

In addition, ask them to mark each store's location on a street map and use a public transportation route map to plan how they will travel from store to store. It is a good idea to have students add the cost of transportation in with their purchases, so that they will hesitate before traveling across town to save a few cents on what appears to be a better buy.

47. Consumer Report

This activity will require your students to do a little comparative shopping. Have work groups, each supplied with a week's worth of newspapers for different weeks, determine the best buys for their week. Have the groups use the following questions and guidelines:

Are there any items that appear to offer substantial reductions in price? Make a list and discuss them with others in your household who are making spending decisions. Note their comments.

Is there a particular category of items that seems to be "on sale"? (For example, linens are traditionally offered at reduced prices in January during "White Sales.")

How can you tell if something is really a good buy?

Students can do some price checking in stores, consult consumer analysis magazines, compare their week's prices with prices other groups may have noted for another week, and find out all they can about the items that appear to be good buys.

When students have gathered the information, discussed it as a group, and reached an agreement on one or two items that seem to represent the best buys, they can clip the ad, write a statement as to why the item is a good buy in the group's opinion, and post the ad on the bulletin board. It should be interesting to note which groups come up with the same recommendations, and which vary.

48. Ads of Another Kind

Students may have noticed that some display ads do not try to sell a product. Some may sell services offered by businesses such as banks or savings and loan companies. Others may present a position on a strike or the political views of a group of people on an issue or a candidate. Each of these ads is nonetheless trying to persuade the reader to do or think something. Have your students complete the following tasks:

1. Search in the collection of newspapers for a display ad that does not mention a product.

2. Clip this ad and paste it on a sheet of notebook paper.

3. Underline the words or phrases that are intended to persuade the reader.

4. Write a statement of what this ad wants the reader to do or think. Discuss why you would or would not be persuaded.

49.   The Silver Screen

Movie ads in newspapers vary a great deal from community to community. Some newspapers have responded to local demands for their standard of decency in film advertising, and other communities have not raised strong objections to explicit sex or violence in movie ads. If you and your class are comfortable with the movie ads that appear in your newspaper, have the students analyze them by answering these questions:

Which of these items is most often used to attract people to G-, PG-, R-, and X rated movies—the director, the cast, the subject matter, or the graphic art work?

How is language used differently to advertise movies of different maturity ratings?

How do the ratings themselves serve as advertisements for movies?

10

CLASSIFIED ADVERTISING
Buying Wisely

Anyone can buy advertising space in the classified ads and try to sell almost anything. It is the place to offer the bike you no longer ride, your dog's litter of puppies, the car you want to replace with a newer model, or the antique lamp in the attic. A two-line ad running for four days will probably cost $12 to $14. The classified ad is an economical way for private individuals to reach a broad market when they want to buy or sell something.

Classified ads are also the place to look when you want to buy. The reader can choose not only from private owner ads, but also from auction house ads, retail merchants' ads, and the ads of others who specialize in handling used, odd-lot, or unusual merchandise.

Buying and selling are an important function of the classified ads, but not the only one. The Help Wanted columns advertise jobs available in the community, and the Position Wanted ads describe people who are looking for specific kinds of work. In addition, the Personals relay messages and requests to private individuals, and the Services describe a variety of home maintenance services available in the community.

Space is usually at a premium for the person placing the ad; so, in order to give the potential buyer the most information in a two- or three-line ad, the seller uses abbreviations freely. The classified ads, particularly in the real estate section, may seem to be written in a language all their own.

SECTION SURVEY

Just for fun, ask your students how many advertising classifications they think there are in the classified section of the newspaper. They will probably greatly underestimate the extent of the section's resources. Distribute one classified section to each student. The issues from which you take the sections should have been published within the same season. After students have browsed through and familiarized themselves with the classified section, ask them to conduct a section survey using the following questions and procedural guidelines:

Classified Advertisements Survey

How many classifications are there in this section? What is the extent of the coverage of classified material? How are ads distributed within the many classifications? How do classified ads differ from display ads?

1.   Count the number of classifications listed in the section. (If consecutive numbers are assigned to each classification, find the last number.)

2.   Using your earlier figure for column inches per page, determine the number of column inches for the entire newspaper and the number of column inches for the classified section alone. Compute the percentage of space per issue devoted to classified ads.

3.   Measure how many column inches of ads are distributed under each classification. Note which classifications carry the most listings. Speculate on how the season affects the distribution. (For example, ads for cars and real estate are generally heavy in the spring, jobs in the fall.)

4.   Compare classified and display advertisements in terms of economy of money and space. List the abbreviations used in classified ads and try to expand them.

After the class has completed the survey, compare and discuss your findings. Keep in mind the questions posed at the beginning of the survey. Your data analysis should provide the answers.

FOLLOW-UP FINDINGS

If the class is working well with visitors from the community, invite a representative of a personal agency, a real estate agent, an auto dealer, or some other business person who regularly advertises in the classified section to come and talk with the class about his or her experiences with this kind of advertising.

Instead, or in addition, have each student conduct a mini-survey on his or her block to find out more from people who have at some time used the classified ads. Each student might plan to interview ten adults on these questions:

Did you ever place an ad in the classified section to sell something?

About how many responses did you receive?

Did you sell the article as a result of the ad?

When students return to class with the results of their surveys, ask them to combine their results to better assess the effectiveness of these ads.

The students can tabulate:

the total number of people interviewed

the percentage who have placed classified ads

of those, the total number of responses and the average number of responses per ad

the percentage of ads that yielded a sale

ASSIGNMENT: Write a Classified Ad

Ask your students to look around the room, select an item or group of items or the room itself, and compose a classified advertisement about it. The ad could also be designed to promote a sale, rental, or summer job opportunity for a student. Or it might involve a service or a skill. Here are two examples:

1.   By students one lvly classrm, std. sz. lg windows. view. immed. poss. resnable.

2.   Help Wanted Student Person w/reading bkgd comb. w/brains + endurance adv. poss. great

Ads can be grouped, alphabetized, or arranged as they are in the newspaper. This entire "Classified Ad" section can be pasted on large sheets and displayed on the bulletin board.

SECTION ACTIVITIES

50.   Newcomers

Have each of your students pretend that he or she is suddenly an adult and has just arrived in town looking for a job and a place to live. Instruct each student to attend to the following:

1.   Study the Help Wanted section in one edition, and select three positions for which to apply.

2.   Write a letter to each potential employer telling why you should be considered for the job and requesting an interview. Older students can also list the kinds of education and experience they think they would need to qualify for each position.

3.   Study the "Apartment for Rent" ads. If a salary figure was included in the job ad the student was interested in, he or she can use it as a guide to selecting affordable apartment rents. If not, the class can discuss rents and agree on a range that might be practical for a single person renting a first apartment. Consider the differences in the sizes of apartments that are available, and decide what would be an ideal size for a single person. Then, survey the range of rent charged for this size unit. Note where apartments of this size and kind are located, and mark the locations on a town map.

If possible arrange for small groups of students to visit two or three vacant apartments with an adult volunteer and a real estate person. Discuss what a person needs to know about an apartment before he or she agrees to rent it. List ten things a person should check out before renting. This list might include information on utilities, trash collection, pets, parking, and lease.

51. Moving In

Students again assume that they are now adults. They have located jobs and apartments, which now need to be furnished. Students may either work with a given amount of cash or, if they are able to handle more computations, a monthly income to be spent over a period of several months on furnishings and other household expenses. In either case, they can use both the display ads and the classifieds to make thier choices. Ask them to:

1.   Make a list of furnishings needed. This will vary widely from person to person.

2.   Look for ads featuring these items.

3.   When an ad sounds good, make this kind of notation: table 2/17 classified used, walnut dropleaf, gd. cond. $40. If a more desirable-sounding table appears in another ad, mark out the original notation and substitute the new one.

Some items may not appear for sale in either the display ads or the classifieds during the period of this activity. General merchandise catalogs can be used to complete the furnishings.

On the final day of the activity, each student will add the figures in the notations to determine the total amount he or she plans to spend. If the amount exceeds the assigned budget, insist that adjustments in spending be made. Suggest that the student set priorities to determine which items can be purchased at another time.

52.   Wheels!

Many students imagining themselves as adults will also fantasize that they own cars, motorcycles, or some other kind of vehicle. Again using a declared salary or income figure, the students can shop for vehicles. As with selecting furnishings, they can use both display and classified ads and consider new and used vehicles.

Older students can look over loan application forms, discuss what the terms mean, and try filling out sample forms using their imaginary businesses, ages, and other information. In assessing their overall, continuing costs in owning a car, students should include gas, oil, insurance, maintenance, parking, and so forth. They can then get figures on insurance costs and calculate the cost per mile for this kind of transportation.

53.   Getting Personal

Among the Personals and other shorter categories in the classified ads there are some very provocative tidbits, which are like vignettes. Ask each student to look over these columns from several editions and select one interesting item to use as the basis for a story.

Remind students that stories *begin* with a situation; *continue* with a problem, controversy, dilemma, or mystery; and *end* with a solution, resolution, or conclusion. If students enjoy using these items as story-starters, they can try writing several each and assembling them in a class anthology of "Personals."

54.   Which Side of the Tracks?

Working in small groups, students can search the ads for information on homes and apartments for sale and rent, and find out how price and location relate to your community.

Have students follow these steps:

1.   Circle all the ads in one edition that give both price and location.

2.   Choose a color for each price grouping, and mark accordingly. For example, under $200 a month rentals—green; $201 to $300 —yellow; and so forth. Similar groupings can also be determined for sale prices.

3.   Use the color indicating cost to make a dot on the town map to show the location.

4.   Determine which areas have mostly lower-priced housing and which have mostly higher. Can you guess why this might be?

5.   Get a copy of a zoning map from your city planning department, and determine what kinds of housing are permitted in each zone and why these zones were created.

11

VITAL STATISTICS
Understanding Facts and Figures

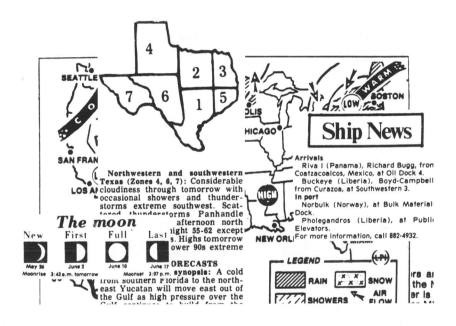

Newspaper editors generally select from among the statistics collected by various agencies in the community those they will publish in their papers. Statistics of this kind are public service features, and editorial policy varies from place to place. But weather statistics are carried by almost all daily papers and usually include temperature, rainfall, snowfall, wind velocities, and cloud cover for the previous day. They also include an extended forecast or prediction. There may also be year-to-date figures, seasonal averages, and data for surrounding towns and even for other cities.

In every community, many kinds of records are noted each day. Births and deaths are recorded, marriage licenses and divorce petitions are filed, legal notices of various kinds are posted, and so forth. In the past these were routinely reported in the daily press too, but today many newspapers no longer print these domestic statistics. Reports of deaths may appear in the form of obituaries or funeral notices, but not commonly in statistical form.

Natural phenomena may be reported along with the weather information, including the times of sunrise, sunset, moonrise, and moonset. Sometimes even the phases of the moon and the dates for each are included. If the town is located near an ocean, tide tables may be published. Port cities will also list ship arrivals and departures. Other regular occurrences of this nature will probably be reported in the newspaper if they are of interest to people in the area.

SECTION SURVEY

Since statistics are provided on quite different subjects, they may appear practically anywhere in the newspaper. Ask your students to look carefully through all the sections and circle every item that appears to be a statistic. At the same time, subdivide the class into work groups and assign each group one week's worth of papers. Then ask the groups to conduct a survey of vital statistics using the following questions and guidelines:

Vital Statistics Survey

What kinds of statistics does your newspaper print? Are there any observable patterns to the coverage? To whom are the statistics useful?

1.   Note the different kinds of statistics printed during the week for which you have papers. Note which statistics appear every day.

2.   Note the days on which occasional statistics are printed. Point out any patterns in terms of arrangement, frequency, and time of the week.

3.   Make general observations about the geographic characteristics, weather-dependent industries and recreation facilities, and population growth in your community. Note which groups are likely to have a strong interest in which statistics. For instance, is ocean fishing an important industry in your town? If so, the newspaper probably prints statistics about the weather fronts and tides which will be of crucial interest to people fishing, boating, or sailing.

After your group has completed the survey, discuss the findings. Keep in mind the questions posed at the beginning of the survey. Your data analysis should provide the answers.

FOLLOW-UP FINDINGS

Students can perform their own weather observations and compare their results with those in the newspaper. Here is a suggested routine that students can perform each day.

1.   Note the cloud cover, if any, for morning, noon, and afternoon.

2.   Record the temperature by reading a thermometer placed out-doors.

3.   Note the precipitation, if any. Measure it, if a measuring device is available.

Other observations can also be made if equipment for measuring wind direction and velocity is accessible. The following day, newspaper statistics or records for each of these items can be checked against the students' observations.

ASSIGNMENT: Write a Statistical Summary

Students can collect some vital statistics themselves and write a brief statistical report. For example, one student can report on class attendance. After answering the following questions, the student should write a summary report:

What percent of enrolled students are in class each day?

What is the average number present (this week)?

Are there noticeable variations in attendance? How can this be explained?

Why would anyone want to know these statistics? Who might use this information?

SECTION ACTIVITIES

55. Rate of Returns

Ask one student to report on the number of books checked out each day at the library. Have another person record the number of books returned. Inquire if the librarian would like your help in encouraging students to either check out more books, return books more promptly, or both. If the answer is yes (and why wouldn't it be?), hold a contest.

Ask your students to draw up a chart showing all the homerooms in your school or all the student groups participating in the contest. Have them post weekly figures for each group showing the total number of books checked out, returned, and overdue. Discuss with your class what effect announcing the statistics had on the circulation of books in the library. If the circulation has increased, discuss how statistics motivate people to compete. (Use the breaking of records in the Olympics as an example.)

56. Sunrise, Sunset

Plan a four- to six-week observation period for charting the sunrise and sunset. Ask your students to design a wall hanging that shows the time pattern of sunrise and sunset according to the statistics provided in the newspaper. Have them follow these steps:

1. Cut out a very large orange circle and divide it into twenty-four equal segments to represent the hours of the day. Label each segment accordingly. Add notches in each to indicate the quarter hour, the half hour, and the three-quarter hour.

2. Cut out a small pink circle and a small purple circle for every day included in your observation period. The pink circles represent the light sun, or the sunrise. The purple circles represent the dark sun, or the sunset.

3. On consecutive Mondays (or whatever weekday you chose), observe the time of the sunrise and sunset for the day to the nearest quarter hour. One student should be appointed to chart this weekly information.

4. At the close of the observation period, study the wall chart and discuss any observable patterns.

Students should note the lengthening of daylight hours between sunrise and sunset during any period between December 22 and June 21, and the shortening of daylight hours between June 22 and December 21. (See the Sunrise/Sunset Wall Chart on page 102.)

If you like, plan a brief astronomy lesson in which you teach students about the winter and summer solstices. Discuss time zones and the reasons for instituting daylight saving time.

57. Moon Patterns

Ask your students to make a similar wall chart to observe the moonrise and moonset. However, note that students need only make their observations for a one- or two-week period since the observations will be made daily, not weekly. Have students follow these steps:

1. Cut out a very large yellow circle and divide it into twenty-four equal segments to represent the hours of the day. Label each segment accordingly. Add notches in each to indicate the quarter hour, the half hour, and the three-quarter hour.

2. Cut out a small pink circle and a small purple circle for every day included in your observation period. The pink circles represent the moonrise; the purple circles represent the moonset.

Sunrise / Sunset Wall Chart

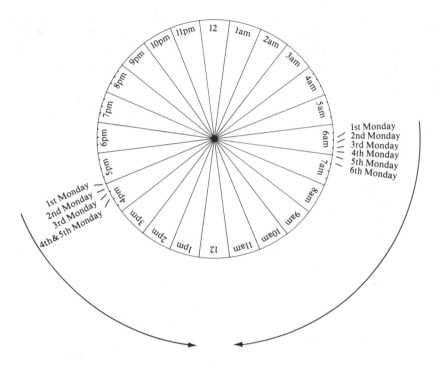

3. On consecutive days for a week or more, observe the time of the moonrise and moonset to the nearest quarter hour. One student should be appointed to chart this daily information.

4. At the close of the observation period, study the wall chart and discuss any observable patterns.

Students should notice the amount of moonlight hours remains nearly the same, but the hours of moonrise and moonset move forward or later in the day. (See Moonrise/Moonset Wall Chart on next page.)

58. Time and Tide

If your community is near the ocean, students can study the tide tables and visit the beach to observe the ebb and flow of the tides. Have your students consider who needs to know when to expect a high tide or a low tide, and how the tide affects the creatures that live on the beach. Some students may want to read about life in tidal pools and report to the class.

Moonrise/Moonset Wall Chart

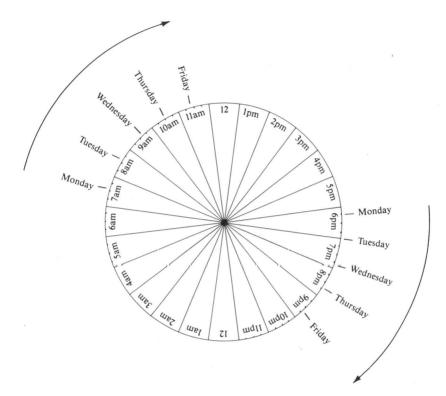

59. Port of Call

If it is convenient, provide several editions of a newspaper from a port city so that students can map the commerce sailing in and out of that port. The students will need a world map, maptacks, and colored yarns for the following activity steps:

1.   On the map, attach one strand of yarn at the port for each ship sailing that day.
2.   Attach the opposite end of the strand to the destination port.
3.   Paste or pin a card along the yarn telling what cargo the ship carries, if that information is given in the newspaper.
4.   Show arriving ships with a different colored yard.

12

THE FUNNY PAGES
Enjoying Comics and Puzzles

Nearly every city newspaper runs six or more comic strips plus three or four single-frame cartoons each day. A crossword puzzle, a word search, or a column about bridge or chess may also be included. The purpose of all of these items is naturally to amuse the reader.

Comic strips usually contain two to four, occasionally five, frames. In some strips the story is complete each day, while in others it is continued from day to day in the form of a serial. The one-day strips are often simply visual jokes in which the first scene depicts a comical situation, the next frame or frames elaborate on it, and the final scene illustrates the punch line. Some of the most common topics of these jokes include the state of current affairs, the plight of humanity in general, or a play on words. Serial comics usually deal with the themes of romance, adventure, superheroes, or science fiction in much the same way as popular novels or television soap operas.

Single-frame cartoons must set up the story and get a chuckle all in one picture. Again, the themes are generally the same as those used in the one-day comic strips. Cartoons are often scattered throughout the newspaper, whereas comic strips are usually grouped together on one or more special pages. Editorial cartoons (see Chapter 4, page 36) should not be included in this study since their primary intent is to comment, not entertain.

SECTION SURVEY

Begin your survey by having students carefully cut out all the comic strips, cartoons, puzzles, and game articles wherever they occur in the paper. By now you should have accumulated enough papers to have each student work alone with an individual issue. The paper date is not important, since the space allotted to these entertainment pages is not likely to vary. Have the students assemble and paste their clippings on a blank sheet of paper so that they can handle them efficiently. When they have done so, ask them to conduct an independent survey of their funny page material using the following questions and procedural guidelines:

Funny Pages Survey

How much space is devoted to funny page material in a day's issue? How does the humor in various comic strips differ? What are the different types of material included in the newspaper for your entertainment?

1.   Figure the total number of column inches in your day's issue of the newspaper. Then measure the column inches devoted to funny

page material that same day. Compute the percentage of space devoted to funny page material.

2.   Note which strips are humorous and which are not. Observe the different kinds of humor. List each humorous strip under a general humor heading, such as Slapstick, Pun, Black Humor, Understatement, Overstatement, Wit, Situation Comedy, or Satire.

3.   Examine the comic strips that do not come under a humor heading; some are dramatic rather than funny. Note whether or not these comics are serials.

4.   Note the other types of literary amusements that the newspaper provides. Then compare your findings with those of the other students. See if you have missed out on any fun!

When the entire class has completed the survey, compare and discuss your findings. Keep in mind the questions posed at the beginning of the survey. Your data analysis should provide the answers.

FOLLOW-UP FINDINGS

Encourage your students to explore the ways in which different kinds of humor appeal to different kinds of people. Have them select a sampling of comic strips that includes one or two from each category of humor they noted in their section surveys. Instruct them to do the following to prepare an interview package:

1.   Tape or paste these strips on a sheet of heavy paper.
2.   Number each strip.
3.   Take several blank sheets of paper so that you can give one to each person interviewed.
4.   Number each sheet from 1 to 6 and write at the bottom 20–30 years old, 31–50 years old, 51–70 years old, over 70 years old.

Tell them to have several adults look at the comics and write after each number *funny, not funny,* or *so-so,* and to indicate to which of the four age groups they belong. After checking with these adults, the student can make a tally of responses to show which strip people found most funny, least funny, and so forth. Have your students compare their findings and discuss these questions:

What relationship is there between age and response to the comic?

Is the response to the survey about what you expected? If not, how does it differ?

ASSIGNMENT: Write Something Humorous

Each student should acquire a joke or funny story, which might come from a TV program, a joke book, or another person. The next step is to write it down so it won't be forgotten. Have the students keep in mind the two to four frame format of comic strips. Ask them to use the following questions as format guides:

What is the situation?

Who is involved?

What happens next?

What is the punch line?

How is the expected outcome changed?

As students are writing out their jokes to fit this format, suggest they visualize symbols or images they might use to tell this funny story. Remind them that there are very few words in most funny comics. Some students may want to count the words in a strip they think is funny and use that figure as a rough guide for the number of words they'll use.

In every class there will be some students who enjoy drawing and are adept at creating pictorial representations. These students may want to draw their comic strips. Others can look for figures already in print to cut out and paste into their comics. Completed strips can be displayed.

SECTION ACTIVITIES

60. Puzzling Puzzles

Divide the class into groups of three or four, and ask each group to select one crossword puzzle. If students have never worked on this kind of puzzle, explain how the clues and words are arranged. Be sure there are dictionaries available.

If students come to a word for which they cannot find a definition, one person can write the word on an index card and post it on the bulletin board. People from other groups may be able to supply a meaning. If a group is stumped on the first puzzle, this group may try a second one, and so on. Answer keys can be used to check progress.

61. Playing the Game

Students can bring in cards or chess sets and set up the playing situations described in a card or chess game article. Interested students can consult game books to learn more about plays for particular moves and situations.

62. A Crossword Guide

After students have tried several crossword puzzles, ask them to identify difficult and unusual words for further study using the following procedure:

1. Write each word you found tricky or unusual on an index card.
2. Write a clue beside each word.

When a number of these cards have been written out, ask a student to arrange them in alphabetical order. Students can refer to these cards and add to the collection as they continue to work on crossword puzzles. The cards will serve as a crossword puzzle dictionary of sorts.

63. What Next?

Selecting only the serial comic strips, students can arrange them in chronological order. At this point in the study, each student may have several weeks' worth of a serial comic strip. Project the series, using an opaque projector, so that everyone can read the strips at the same time. After the viewing, have each student write a sentence or two describing the action he or she predicts will take place in the next day's strip. The next day project the new strip for class viewing. See how the predictions compare.

64.   Is Everything in Order?

If some students are experiencing problems ordering the sequence of events, ask each of them to make a puzzle and trade it with another student:

1.   Paste a one-day comic onto tagboard. Cut carefully around the entire strip.
2.   Cut between each scene. Code the scenes in order on the reverse side.
3.   Make a copy of the code sequence, and keep it in your notebook.
4.   Mix up the scenes, and put them in an envelope with your name on it.
5.   Trade puzzles with another student.

Students should try to arrange the scenes in proper order. Then they turn the scenes over and copy the code numbers as they appear. This code sequence can be checked with the person whose name appears on the envelope.

65.   Where's Orphan Annie?

Have your students ask parents or adults living in their household which comic strips they remember from their childhood. The students can then prepare this information for a class discussion. Pose these questions to guide the discussion:

Are any of the comics mentioned still running in any of the papers the class studied? If so, which ones?

Why have these survived?

Which ones seem to have disappeared? Why might this be so?

Students may want to read biographical material on the careers of certain well-known comic artists like Charles Schultz or Milton Caniff. To conclude the activity, ask:

Which comics will still be printed twenty years from now and why might this be so?

What might the comics of the future be like? Why?

GLOSSARY
Standard Terms

angle: the approach taken in reporting the facts of a news event

article: the full text of a news story or feature

banner or *banner headline:* a large front page headline which some-times spans the full width of the page

bias: a newspaper's or individual's prejudicial stance on an issue which colors the way in which facts are reported or considered

by-line: a line of copy which identifies by name the writer of an article; usually placed at the beginning of an article

caption: the explanatory copy which accompanies a photograph or illustration

cardstacking: the imbalanced or distorted presentation of facts

classified advertising: brief advertisements which are divided into categories or classes and run together in the newspaper

clippings: items cut out of the newspaper

column: a vertical arrangement of copy on a news page; a regular newspaper feature

column inch: a measurement of newspaper space which is one inch deep and one inch wide

commentary: opinionated material which has been written by indi-viduals other than the editors of a newspaper and which does not necessarily reflect the opinion of the newspaper *contributor:* an individual whose writing contribution has been accepted for publication by a newspaper or other periodical

copy: news and other written textual matter which will be typeset and printed in the newspaper

copy edit: to correct errors in style, content, grammar, and spelling in written copy before it is typeset

co-op advertising: ads which are sponsored cooperatively by a national producer and local merchants or distributors

coverage: the frequency and amount of space allotted to a single news item

dateline: the first line of copy under a headline which tells the date and origin of the news report which follows

display advertising: advertising that is set off from newspaper text by larger display typefaces, rules, incorporated white space, and illustrations

ears: information boxes in the top corners of the front page

editor: the individual responsible for management and content of a particular section of the newspaper, or the entire newspaper (in the latter instance, usually called the *editor-in-chief)*

editorial: opinionated material which states the viewpoint of a particular newspaper according to its publisher and/or editors

editorial cartoon: a cartoon which illustrates a newspaper's editorial stance on an issue

fact: that which is verifiable

fair comment: opinion based on facts that are fairly and accurately stated

feature: newspaper material which is not news-oriented

fillers: brief, miscellaneous items used to fill up space in a newspaper

flag: the name and symbol of the newspaper printed in a display typeface across the width of the front page (also called *nameplate*)

front page: the first sheet or section of a newspaper which is devoted to the most newsworthy stories of the day

headline: larger display type which serves as a title for the copy below *index:* the feature box found usually on the front page which lists a newspaper's contents and corresponding pages, and sections and section codes

interview: a meeting between a reporter and a newsworthy individual in order for the reporter to obtain first-hand information; a question-and-answer format for reporting information obtained directly from sources, or a format which makes prolific use of quotes obtained in an interview with a newsworthy or interesting personality

inverted pyramid: the journalistic format for organizing and writing straight news articles in which details are reported in descending order of importance

journalist: a writer or editor for the news media

journalism: the acquisition, writing, and dissemination of news information

layout: the arrangement of items on a publication page

lead or *lead-in:* the first sentence of a news story

lead story: the most important front page story found under the banner headline and usually allocated the most extensive coverage

masthead: the feature box found usually on the editorial page which includes the name of the publisher, editor(s), time and place of publication, and subscription information

nameplate: see *flag.*

news: current factual information which is of immediate relevance to readers and viewers of communications media

news analysis: a form of commentary in which a writer scrutinizes the facts of a news event, suggests various implications, raises issues, and assesses the significance of activity generated by that news event

news conference: the collective meeting of representatives of the press with a newsworthy individual in order for that individual to disseminate information; the individual will usually make an announcement and/or entertain questions from the assembled press persons

opinion: that which cannot be verified as fact

photo-journalism: journalism which emphasizes photographic depictions of news events rather than prose recountings of them *proofread:* to read copy which has been typeset for errors in spelling, punctuation, and typography

reliable sources: anonymous individuals who provide reporters with informational tips which are accurate; often these individuals are in positions of authority or have access to secret information

reporter: an individual who amasses, organizes, and writes news articles based on facts

reportorial style: the formal, factual style of reporting the news

scope: the extent to which a news item is regionally and topically relevant to readers or viewers

staff reporter/writer: a writer or reporter who receives assignments from and works directly for a particular newspaper

straight news: news which is characterized by reportorial style and organized according to the inverted pyramid format

syndication: a business organization which sells articles written by popular or controversial journalists to many periodic publications such as newspapers and magazines to be published simultaneously

wire service: a news agency which transmits syndicated news copy by teletype to subscribers such as newspapers and broadcast networks

ACTIVITY INDEX

SKILL-BUILDERS AND LONG-TERM PROJECTS

1. Find Your Way Around   14
2. Where in the World?   15
3. Spider and Fly   15
4. Word Watching: Synonyms   15
5. Word Watching: Vocabulary   16
6. Dictionary Update   16
7. Captive Captions   17
8. Series Reports   17
9. Political Profiles   18

THE FRONT PAGE

10. Making the Front Page   26
11. A Measure of Importance   27
12. Tour a Newspaper Office   27
13. History in the Making   28
14. Past Pages   28
15. Secondhand History   29
16. Weather Watch   29
17. What's at Stake?   29
18. It's All in Your Point of View!   30

EDITORIALS AND COMMENTARY

19. Cartoon Commentary   36
20. Dear Editor   37

21. Yours Truly   38

22. Analysis of an Analysis   38

23. Who's Who Among the Editors   38

24. Let's Face Facts   39

COMMUNITY NEWS

25. Who Counts?   46

26. Where Is It All Happening?   47

27. Who Can Afford It?   47

28. A Scholarly View   47

THE BUSINESS WORLD

29. Charting the Market   54

30. Bulls and Bears: The Influence of Historic
     Events on the Market   55

31. Investing in the Stock Market   57

32. A Dollar Here, A Dollar There   58

33. Balancing Trade   59

34. More Trading   59

35. Keeping Up with Inflation   60

SPORTS SCENE

36. Sports Talk   65

37. Retrospect in Sports   65

38. What Are the Odds?   66

39. Series Standings   66

40. Most Valuable Player   68

41. Men Only?   69

NEWSPAPER FEATURES

42. Some Leg Work   76

43. All Ticketed Passengers!   77

44. Dear Doctor   78

45. Class Cookbook   79

DISPLAY ADVERTISING

46. Shopping Spree   85

47. Consumer Report   86

48. Ads of Another Kind   86

49. The Silver Screen   87

CLASSIFIED ADVERTISING
    50. Newcomers   92
    51. Moving In   93
    52. Wheels!   94
    53. Getting Personal   94
    54. Which Side of the Tracks?   94

VITAL STATISTICS
    55. Rate of Returns   100
    56. Sunrise, Sunset   101
    57. Moon Patterns   101
    58. Time and Tide   102
    59. Port of Call   103

THE FUNNY PAGES
    60. Puzzling Puzzles   109
    61. Playing the Game   109
    62. A Crossword Guide   109
    63. What Next?   109
    64. Is Everything in Order?   110
    65. Where's Orphan Annie?   110

About the Authors

J. Rodney Short, Ed.D., and Bev Dickerson are well-known in Texas and adjacent states for their work with teachers focusing on classroom uses of the newspaper. Operating both as a team and independently, Dr. Short and Ms. Dickerson emphasize in their workshops the range of objectives, both educational and motivational, which can be realized through newspaper-based activities. Dr. Short is associate professor of education and associate dean at Texas Women's University, Denton. Ms. Dickerson is presently manager of Newspaper in Education, **Corpus Christi Caller-Times.** Her career spans NIE positions with a number of major newspapers.

Fearon Teacher Aids...

Motivating Today's Students—disaffected, disinterested students can be reached. Based on the experience of veteran teachers, this LEARNING handbook deals with specific motivational problems and describes successful strategies to help your students become motivated achievers. Content includes games and activities that help students understand their need to achieve, and motivational techniques for you to use in one-to-one relationships. **Motivating Today's Students** by Walter F. Drew, Anita R. Olds, and Henry R. Olds, Jr.: 96 pages; 5½" x 8½"; illustrated; paperbound; 1908-4

How do you turn your teens on to learning? **Turn-Ons!** offers you scores of workable, imaginative solutions to the problem of student motivation. Stressing interaction with positive feedback, these strategies are arranged in a developmental order under five unit headings: Class Starters, Social Psychology, Social Problems, Historical Methodology, and American Government. You can easily adapt most of them for use in several curriculum areas. **TURN-ONS! 185 Strategies for the Secondary Classroom** by Stephen K. Smuin: 208 pages; 6" x 9"; paperbound; 7051-9

A practical approach to help students understand who they are, who they'd like to be, and how to become more like their ideal selves. **Developing Individual Values in the Classroom** provides down-to-earth activities to help you develop every child's own values. Content includes discussions of key valuing concepts; directions for value-discovery activities; and games and other self-diagnosing projects that help students examine their lives, feelings, and goals. **Developing Individual Values in the Classroom** by Richard L. Curwin and Geri Curwin: 96 pages; 5½" x 8½"; illustrated; paperbound; 1902-5

the Idea Books that Free You to Teach

Word Games offers you 19 enjoyable games—complete with word lists and lively applications—to help your elementary students become more conscious of words and express themselves more effectively. The book also features ideas for making duplicating masters. **Word Games** by Niels Grant, Jr.: 80 pages; 5⅜" x 8⅜"; paperbound; 7485-9

Spelling Games and Puzzles for Junior High helps build your students' basic competence in a creative, enjoyable way. Two games on duplicatable MAKEMASTER® activity sheets accompany each of these 24 spelling lists. Recommended by *Teacher.* **Spelling Games and Puzzles for Junior High** by Robert D. Miller: 88 perforated pages; 8½" x 11"; illustrated; paperbound; 6460-8

Hands-On Grammar is an indispensable list of grammatical definitions with examples for teachers, students, writers, executives—*anyone* who needs to know. **Hands-On Grammar: An Instant Resource** by Stan Laird: 48 pages; 5½" x 8½"; paperbound; 3255-2

Developing Skills in Critical Reading provides many projects for improving reading comprehension. It contains activities that use classroom teaching materials in innovative ways, as well as detailing many activities using spoken language, cartoons, photographs, and advertisements. By using the activities in this book, you'll help students recognize and deal with facts, opinions, and messages. **Developing Skills in Critical Reading** by Beth S. Atwood: 96 pages; 5½" x 8½"; illustrated; paperbound; 1903-3

New For the 1980s!

1, 2, 3, Read! is the book you need if your friend, your student, or your child has not yet broken this crucial learning barrier—and nobody but you is really going to help. You don't have to be a specialist; you don't have to know any fancy words. You *do* have to care, and apply the simple, no-nonsense techniques in this book. **1, 2, 3, READ! A Step-by-Step Tutoring Plan for Teachers, Parents, and Friends** by Judith Dettre: 128 pages; 6″ x 9″; 5788-1

In **Look It Up!**, you'll find a wealth of classroom-tested, skill-building activities to help your students use the dictionary more effectively. Many activities relate to a variety of subject areas. Your kids will enjoy learning the features of the dictionary as they expand their general knowledge and communication skills. **LOOK IT UP! 101 Dictionary Activites to Develop Word Skills** by Nicholas P. Criscuolo: 72 pages; 5½″ x 8½″; illustrated; paperbound; 4330-9

Yes you *can* bridge the gap between the pocket calculator and the mathematics you want to teach. **Calculator Math** tells you how. This three-book MAKEMASTER® series shows your students that effective calculator use depends on their careful consideration of a problem's structure, their imaginative search for strategies, their feeling for magnitudes, and their growing mathematical insight. Each book features highly motivating, duplicatable activity sheets, answer pages, and a teacher's guide. **Calculator Math** by Gerardus Vervoort and Dale Mason: 8½″ x 11″ each; paperbound.

Beginning (grades 5–7): 96 perforated pages; 1200-4
Intermediate (grades 6–8): 96 perforated pages; 1201-2
Advanced (grades 8–10): 88 perforated pages; 1202-0

Fearon Teacher Aids
P.O. Box 280
Carthage, Illinois 62321